SYSTEMATIC THEOLOGY

An Exploration of Christian Doctrine

Dr. Maxwell Shimba

Printed in the United States of America

TABLE OF CONTENTS

INTRODUCTION TO SYSTEMATIC THEOLOGY

Systematic theology is an essential discipline within Christian studies, offering a structured and coherent approach to understanding the vast and profound truths of the Christian faith. This book aims to provide a comprehensive overview of key doctrines, helping believers deepen their knowledge of God, strengthen their faith, and live out their calling with greater clarity and conviction.

What is Systematic Theology?

Systematic theology involves the collection, organization, and presentation of biblical teachings on various topics, seeking to articulate the faith in a coherent and logical manner. Unlike biblical theology, which traces the development of theological themes throughout the Bible, systematic theology arranges these themes topically, providing a holistic view of the Christian doctrine.

The Purpose of Systematic Theology

The primary purpose of systematic theology is to help believers understand the core beliefs of the Christian faith in a structured way. This discipline seeks to answer fundamental questions about God, humanity, salvation, the church, and the future, drawing from the entirety of Scripture to present a unified understanding of these doctrines.

1. To Know God More Deeply

One of the foremost goals of systematic theology is to deepen our knowledge of God. By studying His nature, attributes, and works, we can grow in our appreciation of His greatness and goodness. This knowledge is not merely intellectual but is intended to transform our hearts and lives, leading us to worship and serve Him more faithfully.

2. To Defend the Faith

Systematic theology also equips believers to defend their faith against false teachings and misunderstandings. By clearly articulating what the Bible teaches on various topics, believers can stand firm in their convictions and engage effectively with challenges and questions from both within and outside the church.

3. To Apply Biblical Truth

A thorough understanding of systematic theology helps believers apply biblical truths to their lives. This application is not limited to personal spirituality but extends to all areas of life, including relationships, work, and societal engagement. The doctrines we study should inform and shape our daily living, reflecting the transformative power of the gospel.

4. To Promote Unity in the Church

Systematic theology fosters unity within the body of Christ by providing a common foundation of belief. When believers share a clear understanding of core doctrines, it strengthens their fellowship and collaboration in ministry. This unity is essential for the church's witness to the world, demonstrating the love and truth of Christ.

The Structure of This Book

This book is organized into ten chapters, each dedicated to exploring a key area of systematic theology. These chapters cover the following topics:

1. The Doctrine of Revelation: Examining how God reveals Himself to humanity through general and special revelation.

2. The Doctrine of God: Exploring the nature, attributes, and works of God, including the Trinity.

3. The Doctrine of Christ: Delving into the person and work of Jesus Christ, His incarnation, atonement, and resurrection.

4. The Doctrine of the Holy Spirit: Understanding the person and work of the Holy Spirit in the life of believers and the church.

5. The Doctrine of Humanity: Analyzing the nature, purpose, and destiny of human beings from a biblical perspective.

6. The Doctrine of Salvation: Explaining the process of salvation, including election, justification, sanctification, and glorification.

7. The Doctrine of the Church: Investigating the nature, purpose, and mission of the church.

8. The Doctrine of Last Things: Exploring eschatological themes, including the second coming of Christ, the resurrection of the dead, the final judgment, and the new heavens and new earth.

9. The Practical Implications: Discuss how systematic theology influences Christian living, worship, and mission.

10. Conclusion: Summarizing the importance of systematic theology and encouraging ongoing theological study and application.

The Importance of Studying Systematic Theology

Engaging in systematic theology is not merely an academic exercise; it is a vital practice for every believer. By systematically studying the doctrines of the faith, we can:

- Deepen Our Relationship with God: Understanding who God is and what He has done fosters a closer relationship with Him, grounded in awe, love, and gratitude.

- Strengthen Our Faith: A well-grounded faith is less likely to be shaken by doubts or external challenges. Systematic theology provides a firm foundation for our beliefs.

- Enhance Our Witness: Clear and coherent articulation of the Christian faith enables us to share the gospel more effectively with others.

- Live Faithfully: Applying theological truths to our lives helps us live in a manner that honors God and reflects His character.

Conclusion

The journey of studying systematic theology is both intellectually enriching and spiritually transformative. It invites us to explore the depths of God's revelation, to grow in our understanding of His purposes, and to live out our faith with conviction and clarity. As we embark on this journey together, may we be led to a deeper love for God and a more faithful witness to His grace and truth.

I invite you to engage with the following chapters with an open heart and mind, ready to delve into the profound truths of the Christian faith and to allow these truths to transform your life. Let us begin this journey of theological exploration and discover together the richness of God's revelation to us.

Dr. Maxwell Shimba

Shimba Theological Institute

DR. MAXWELL SHIMBA

CHAPTER 01

INTRODUCTION TO SYSTEMATIC THEOLOGY

1.1 Definition and Purpose of Systematic Theology

Systematic theology is the discipline that aims to organize and articulate the doctrines of the Christian faith in a coherent and comprehensive manner. It seeks to summarize the teachings of the Bible on various theological topics, presenting a unified and systematic overview of Christian beliefs. This field of study is essential for understanding the foundational truths of Christianity and for applying these truths to all areas of life.

Systematic theology differs from other theological disciplines in its method and scope. While biblical theology traces the progressive revelation of God's truth through the historical narrative of the Bible, systematic theology collects and synthesizes the entirety of Scripture to address specific doctrinal questions. It provides a framework for understanding how individual doctrines interrelate and how they apply to the life of the church and the believer.

The purpose of systematic theology is multifaceted:

- To Educate: It teaches believers about the essential doctrines of the faith, helping them to grow in knowledge and spiritual maturity.

- To Defend: It equips believers to defend their faith against false teachings and to articulate their beliefs clearly and accurately.

- To Apply: It guides believers in applying biblical truths to their personal lives, church practices, and interactions with the world.

1.2 The Necessity of Systematic Theology

Systematic theology is necessary for several reasons:

- Biblical Command: Scripture itself calls for believers to grow in the knowledge of God (Colossians 1:10, 2 Peter 3:18). Systematic theology helps fulfill this command by providing a structured way to study and understand biblical doctrines.

- Doctrinal Clarity: By systematically organizing and examining the teachings of the Bible, systematic theology clarifies essential doctrines and helps to prevent misunderstandings and errors.

- Spiritual Growth: A deep understanding of Christian doctrine fosters spiritual growth, as believers come to know God more intimately and live out their faith more faithfully.

- Church Unity: A shared understanding of key doctrines promotes unity within the body of Christ, as believers can stand together on common theological ground.

- Cultural Engagement: Systematic theology equips believers to engage thoughtfully and effectively with the cultural and intellectual challenges of their time, presenting a coherent and compelling Christian worldview.

1.3 Methodology of Systematic Theology

The methodology of systematic theology involves several key steps:

1.3.1 Collection of Biblical Data

The first step is to collect relevant biblical passages that address the theological topic under consideration. This involves a careful exegesis of Scripture, examining the original languages, historical context, and literary genre to understand the intended meaning of the text.

1.3.2 Synthesis of Biblical Teaching

Next, the theologian synthesizes the collected data, organizing it into coherent categories. This involves identifying key themes, drawing connections between different passages, and summarizing the overall biblical teaching on the topic.

1.3.3 Formulation of Doctrines

The synthesized biblical data is then formulated into clear and precise doctrinal statements. These statements should be faithful to the entirety of Scripture, avoiding both under- and over-emphasis of particular texts.

1.3.4 Historical Consideration

Systematic theology also takes into account the historical development of doctrine. This involves studying how key doctrines have been understood and articulated throughout church history, learning from the insights and errors of past theologians.

1.3.5 Interaction with Philosophy and Science

While Scripture is the ultimate authority in systematic theology, theologians also interact with philosophical and scientific insights. This helps to address contemporary questions and challenges, integrating biblical truths with broader knowledge.

1.3.6 Application to Life

Finally, systematic theology seeks to apply doctrinal truths to the life of the believer and the church. This involves ethical considerations, practical theology, and spiritual formation, ensuring that doctrine informs and transforms daily living.

1.4 Major Areas of Systematic Theology

Systematic theology covers a wide range of topics, each addressing a different aspect of the Christian faith. Some of the major areas include:

1.4.1 Theology Proper (The Doctrine of God)

This area focuses on the nature, attributes, and works of God. It includes the study of the Trinity, the character of God, and His actions in creation and providence.

1.4.2 Christology (The Doctrine of Christ)

Christology examines the person and work of Jesus Christ. It explores His divinity and humanity, His incarnation, atoning death, resurrection, and ascension.

1.4.3 Pneumatology (The Doctrine of the Holy Spirit)

Pneumatology studies the person and work of the Holy Spirit. It addresses the Spirit's role in regeneration, sanctification, and empowerment for ministry.

1.4.4 Anthropology (The Doctrine of Humanity)

Anthropology deals with the nature and purpose of human beings. It examines the creation of humanity in the image of God, the fall into sin, and the implications of human sinfulness.

1.4.5 Soteriology (The Doctrine of Salvation)

Soteriology explores how God saves individuals from sin and its consequences. It includes the study of election, justification, sanctification, and glorification.

1.4.6 Ecclesiology (The Doctrine of the Church)

Ecclesiology examines the nature and purpose of the church. It addresses the church's mission, governance, sacraments, and its role in God's redemptive plan.

1.4.7 Eschatology (The Doctrine of Last Things)

Eschatology focuses on the ultimate destiny of individuals and the world. It includes the study of the second coming of Christ, the resurrection of the dead, the final judgment, and the new heavens and new earth.

1.5 Challenges in Systematic Theology

While systematic theology is a vital discipline, it faces several challenges:

1.5.1 The Complexity of Scripture

The Bible is a complex and diverse collection of writings. Systematic theology must carefully balance the various genres, historical contexts, and theological themes present in Scripture.

1.5.2 The Influence of Tradition

Tradition plays a significant role in shaping theological understanding. While tradition can provide valuable insights, systematic theologians must ensure that their conclusions are grounded in Scripture, not merely in historical consensus.

1.5.3 The Need for Humility

Systematic theology requires a humble approach, recognizing the limitations of human understanding. Theologians must be open to correction and willing to revise their conclusions in light of further study and dialogue.

1.5.4 The Tension Between Unity and Diversity

Christian theology encompasses a wide range of perspectives and interpretations. Systematic theology seeks to present a unified understanding of doctrine while respecting the diversity of thought within the broader Christian community.

1.6 Conclusion

Systematic theology is a vital discipline that helps believers understand, articulate, and apply the core doctrines of the Christian faith. By organizing and synthesizing the teachings of the Bible, systematic theology provides a coherent and comprehensive framework for understanding God's truth. As believers engage with systematic theology, they grow in their knowledge of God, deepen their faith, and are better equipped to live out their calling in the world.

In the chapters that follow, we will explore the major areas of systematic theology in greater detail, examining the biblical, historical, and practical dimensions of each doctrine. Our journey will lead us to a deeper appreciation of the richness and depth of the Christian faith, and to a more profound understanding of the God we serve.

DEFINITION AND SCOPE

Systematic theology involves the collection and analysis of biblical teachings to present a unified understanding of core Christian doctrines. It covers areas such as the nature of God, the work of Christ, the role of the Holy Spirit, the nature of humanity, and the purpose of the church. The discipline aims to synthesize the diverse and sometimes complex teachings of the Bible into a coherent system that is both comprehensive and accessible.

By organizing these teachings systematically, theologians can provide clarity and structure to the Christian faith, making it easier for believers to understand and articulate their beliefs. This structured approach helps to highlight the interconnections between different doctrines, showing how they support and illuminate one another. For example, understanding the doctrine of God's nature provides a foundation for comprehending the significance of Christ's work and the Holy Spirit's role in the believer's life.

Systematic theology is not merely an academic exercise; it has practical implications for faith and practice. By studying theology systematically, believers can develop a well-rounded and robust faith that is able to withstand challenges and engage with contemporary issues. This comprehensive understanding aids in spiritual growth, ethical decision-making, and effective ministry.

Moreover, systematic theology helps to guard against doctrinal error and heresy. By clearly defining and explaining the core beliefs of Christianity, it provides a benchmark against which new teachings and interpretations can be measured. This protective function is crucial in maintaining the purity and integrity of the faith, especially in a world where competing ideologies and false teachings abound.

Systematic theology also serves as a bridge between the Bible and the contemporary world. By applying timeless biblical truths to modern questions and challenges, it helps believers to live out their faith in relevant and meaningful ways. This application is not a superficial adaptation, but a deep engagement that seeks to understand how the eternal truths of Scripture speak to today's issues.

In the context of the global church, systematic theology fosters unity by providing a common framework for understanding the Christian faith. Despite cultural and denominational differences, believers can find common ground in the shared doctrines of Christianity. This unity is essential for the church's witness in the world, demonstrating the oneness of the body of Christ.

The scope of systematic theology is vast, encompassing various branches of theological inquiry. These branches include:

- Theology Proper (The Doctrine of God): This branch focuses on understanding the nature and attributes of God, including His omnipotence, omniscience, omnipresence, holiness, love, and justice. It explores the concept of the Trinity and the relationship between the Father, Son, and Holy Spirit.

- Christology (The Doctrine of Christ): Christology examines the person and work of Jesus Christ, including His incarnation, atoning death, resurrection, and ascension. It addresses questions about His divinity and humanity, and His role as Savior and Lord.

- Pneumatology (The Doctrine of the Holy Spirit): This branch studies the person and work of the Holy Spirit, including His role in regeneration, sanctification, and empowerment for service. It explores the gifts and fruit of the Spirit and the Spirit's role in the life of the believer and the church.

- Anthropology (The Doctrine of Humanity): Anthropology addresses the nature and purpose of human beings, including their creation in the image of God, the effects of the fall, and the nature of sin. It explores human destiny and the hope of resurrection.

- Soteriology (The Doctrine of Salvation): Soteriology examines the process and means of salvation, including election, justification, sanctification, and glorification. It explores the role of faith, grace, and the work of Christ in the salvation of individuals.

- Ecclesiology (The Doctrine of the Church): Ecclesiology studies the nature, purpose, and structure of the church. It explores the church's mission, the sacraments, church governance, and the role of the church in God's redemptive plan.

- Eschatology (The Doctrine of Last Things): Eschatology addresses the ultimate destiny of individuals and the world, including the second coming of Christ, the resurrection of the dead, the final judgment, and the new heavens and new earth.

Each of these branches contributes to a holistic understanding of the Christian faith. Together, they form a cohesive system that reflects the richness and depth of biblical revelation. As we delve into the study of systematic theology, we will explore each of these areas in greater detail, seeking to understand how they interconnect and what they reveal about God and His purposes for creation.

In summary, systematic theology is a vital discipline that helps believers to understand, articulate, and live out the core doctrines of the Christian faith. It provides clarity, guards against error, fosters unity, and bridges the gap between biblical truth and contemporary life. By studying theology systematically, we can deepen our knowledge of God, strengthen our faith, and better fulfill our calling as His people.

1.2 The Necessity of Systematic Theology

Systematic theology is indispensable for a robust and well-grounded Christian faith. It fulfills several crucial roles in the life of believers and the church.

Firstly, systematic theology is essential for doctrinal clarity. The Bible, while clear in its overall message, presents its teachings across various genres, contexts, and historical settings. Systematic theology helps to distill these diverse teachings into clear and concise doctrinal statements. For instance, the doctrine of the Trinity is not laid out in a single passage but is derived from the consistent biblical witness to the Father, Son, and Holy Spirit. Systematic theology collects and organizes these scriptural insights, providing a clear understanding of complex doctrines.

Secondly, systematic theology aids in spiritual growth. Understanding the deep truths of the faith can transform how believers live and think. It shapes their worldview, guiding their actions and decisions. For example, a proper understanding of God's sovereignty can bring comfort and assurance in times of trial, knowing that God is in control and works all things for the good of those who love Him (Romans 8:28).

Thirdly, systematic theology is vital for defending the faith. In a world where Christianity is often challenged by alternative worldviews and philosophies, believers need to be equipped to defend their beliefs. Systematic theology provides the intellectual tools to engage with these challenges thoughtfully and respectfully. By understanding the coherent and rational basis of their faith, Christians can more effectively witness to the truth of the gospel.

Furthermore, systematic theology promotes church unity. Despite denominational differences, there are core doctrines that all Christians share. Systematic theology identifies and articulates these shared beliefs, fostering unity within the body of Christ. This unity is essential for the church's witness, demonstrating the love and harmony that should characterize God's people.

Lastly, systematic theology helps believers to engage with contemporary issues. Theological truths are not just historical or abstract; they have practical implications for today's world. For example, a biblical understanding of human dignity can inform Christian responses to social issues such as poverty, injustice, and human rights. Systematic theology helps believers to apply the timeless truths of Scripture to the pressing issues of their time.

In conclusion, systematic theology is a vital discipline that provides clarity, fosters growth, equips for defense, promotes unity, and enables contemporary engagement. As we continue our study, we will explore how these benefits unfold in the various areas of theological inquiry.

1.3 Methodology of Systematic Theology

The methodology of systematic theology involves several key steps, each contributing to the construction of a coherent and comprehensive theological system.

1.3.1 Collection of Biblical Data

The first step is the collection of relevant biblical data. This involves a thorough exegesis of Scripture, examining the original languages, historical context, and literary genres. Exegesis seeks to uncover the intended meaning of the biblical text, ensuring that theological conclusions are grounded in the accurate interpretation of Scripture.

1.3.2 Synthesis of Biblical Teaching

Once the biblical data is collected, the next step is to synthesize this information into coherent categories. This involves identifying key themes and drawing connections between different passages. For example, synthesizing the biblical teaching on salvation involves examining texts from both the Old and New Testaments, and understanding how they contribute to the overall doctrine of salvation.

1.3.3 Formulation of Doctrines

The synthesized biblical data is then formulated into clear and precise doctrinal statements. These statements should be faithful to the entirety of Scripture, avoiding both under- and over-emphasis of particular texts. Formulating doctrines involves careful theological reflection, ensuring that each doctrine accurately reflects the biblical witness.

1.3.4 Historical Consideration

Systematic theology also takes into account the historical development of doctrine. This involves studying how key doctrines have been understood and articulated throughout church history. Historical theology provides valuable insights and helps to avoid repeating past errors. It also shows how the church has responded to various challenges and controversies over time.

1.3.5 Interaction with Philosophy and Science

While Scripture is the ultimate authority in systematic theology, theologians also interact with philosophical and scientific insights. This helps to address contemporary questions and challenges, integrating biblical truths with broader knowledge. For example, engaging with philosophical concepts can help to clarify and defend the rational coherence of Christian doctrines.

1.3.6 Application to Life

Finally, systematic theology seeks to apply doctrinal truths to the life of the believer and the church. This involves ethical considerations, practical theology, and spiritual formation. Doctrine is not just theoretical; it has practical implications for how believers live, worship, and serve. Systematic theology helps to bridge the gap between belief and practice, ensuring that theological truths shape and transform everyday life.

In conclusion, the methodology of systematic theology involves collecting and analyzing biblical data, synthesizing and formulating doctrines, considering historical developments, engaging with philosophy and science, and applying theology to life. This comprehensive approach ensures that systematic theology is grounded in Scripture, informed by tradition, relevant to contemporary issues, and practical for Christian living.

1.4 Major Areas of Systematic Theology

Systematic theology covers a wide range of topics, each addressing a different aspect of the Christian faith. Some of the major areas include:

1.4.1 Theology Proper (The Doctrine of God)

This area focuses on understanding the nature and attributes of God, including His omnipotence, omniscience, omnipresence, holiness, love, and justice. It explores the concept of the Trinity and the relationship between the Father, Son, and Holy Spirit. The study of God's nature provides a foundation for all other theological inquiries.

1.4.2 Christology (The Doctrine of Christ)

Christology examines the person and work of Jesus Christ, including His incarnation, atoning death, resurrection, and ascension. It addresses questions about His divinity and humanity, and His role as Savior and Lord. Understanding Christ's work is central to the Christian faith, as it is through Him that believers are reconciled to God.

1.4.3 Pneumatology (The Doctrine of the Holy Spirit)

Pneumatology studies the person and work of the Holy Spirit, including His role in regeneration, sanctification, and empowerment for service. It explores the gifts and fruit of the Spirit and the Spirit's role in the life of the believer and the church. The Holy Spirit is essential for the Christian life, providing guidance, comfort, and power.

1.4.4 Anthropology (The Doctrine of Humanity)

Anthropology addresses the nature and purpose of human beings, including their creation in the image of God, the effects of the fall, and the nature of sin. It explores human destiny and the hope of resurrection. Understanding humanity's nature and purpose is crucial for addressing questions of identity, morality, and redemption.

1.4.5 Soteriology (The Doctrine of Salvation)

Soteriology examines the process and means of salvation, including election, justification, sanctification, and glorification. It explores the role of faith, grace, and the work of Christ in the salvation of individuals. Salvation is the central theme of the Bible, and understanding its dynamics is vital for the Christian faith.

1.4.6 Ecclesiology (The Doctrine of the Church)

Ecclesiology studies the nature, purpose, and structure of the church. It explores the church's mission, the sacraments, church governance, and the role of the church in

God's redemptive plan. The church is the community of believers, called to worship God and witness to the world.

1.4.7 Eschatology (The Doctrine of Last Things)

Eschatology addresses the ultimate destiny of individuals and the world, including the second coming of Christ, the resurrection of the dead, the final judgment, and the new heavens and new earth. It provides hope and perspective on the future, encouraging believers to live in the light of eternity.

Each of these branches contributes to a holistic understanding of the Christian faith. Together, they form a cohesive system that reflects the richness and depth of biblical revelation. As we delve into the study of systematic theology, we will explore each of these areas in greater detail, seeking to understand how they interconnect and what they reveal about God and His purposes for creation.

1.5 Challenges in Systematic Theology

While systematic theology is a vital discipline, it faces several challenges:

1.5.1 The Complexity of Scripture

The Bible is a complex and diverse collection of writings. Systematic theology must carefully balance the various genres, historical contexts, and theological themes present in Scripture. This complexity requires diligent study and thoughtful synthesis to avoid misinterpretation and to present a coherent theological system.

1.5.2 The Influence of Tradition

Tradition plays a significant role in shaping theological understanding. While tradition can provide valuable insights, systematic theologians must ensure that their conclusions are grounded in Scripture, not merely in historical consensus. This requires a critical engagement with tradition, appreciating its contributions while remaining faithful to the biblical text.

1.5.3 The Need for Humility

Systematic theology requires a humble approach, recognizing the limitations of human understanding. Theologians must be open to correction and willing to revise their conclusions in light of further study and dialogue. This humility fosters a spirit of learning and growth, acknowledging that theology is an ongoing pursuit of truth.

1.5.4 The Tension Between Unity and Diversity

Christian theology encompasses a wide range of perspectives and interpretations. Systematic theology seeks to present a unified understanding of doctrine while respecting the diversity of thought within the broader Christian community. This tension requires careful navigation, balancing the need for doctrinal clarity with an appreciation for legitimate differences.

1.6 Conclusion

Systematic theology is a vital discipline that helps believers to understand, articulate, and live out the core doctrines of the Christian faith. It provides clarity, guards against error, fosters unity, and bridges the gap between biblical truth and contemporary life. By studying theology systematically, we can deepen our knowledge of God, strengthen our faith, and better fulfill our calling as His people.

In the chapters that follow, we will explore the major areas of systematic theology in greater detail, examining the biblical, historical, and practical dimensions of each doctrine. Our journey will lead us to a deeper appreciation of the richness and depth of the Christian faith, and to a more profound understanding of the God we serve.

CHAPTER 02

THE DOCTRINE OF REVELATION

2.1 Introduction to Revelation

The doctrine of revelation is concerned with how God communicates His will and truth to humanity. It forms the foundation upon which all other doctrines are built, as it addresses the essential question of how we can know anything about God. Without revelation, humanity would be left to speculation and uncertainty regarding the nature and purposes of God. Revelation ensures that the knowledge of God is accessible, clear, and reliable.

Revelation is the act of God disclosing Himself and His will to His creation. This self-disclosure comes in various forms and is intended to lead humanity into a relationship with Him. Understanding revelation is crucial for understanding all other aspects of Christian theology, as it provides the means through which God's truths are made known to us.

2.2 General Revelation

General revelation refers to the knowledge of God available to all people through nature, history, and the inner moral law. It is called "general" because it is universally accessible and does not rely on special or supernatural means of communication.

2.2.1 Revelation through Nature

Nature is a primary means of general revelation. The created world reflects the power, wisdom, and goodness of God. Psalm 19:1-4 declares, "The heavens declare the glory of God; the skies proclaim the work of His hands. Day after day they pour forth speech; night after night they reveal knowledge." Similarly, Romans 1:20 states, "For since the creation of the world God's invisible qualities—His eternal power and divine nature—have been clearly seen, being understood from what has been made, so that people are without excuse."

The natural world, with its complexity, order, and beauty, points to a Creator who is powerful and wise. This form of revelation is continuous and available to everyone, providing a universal testimony to God's existence and attributes.

2.2.2 Revelation through History

History is another avenue of general revelation. The unfolding of historical events reveals God's sovereign governance over the affairs of the world. Acts 17:26-27 speaks to this: "From one man He made all the nations, that they should inhabit the whole earth; and He marked out their appointed times in history and the boundaries of their lands. God did this so that they would seek Him and perhaps reach out for Him and find Him, though He is not far from any one of us."

The providential direction of history, the rise and fall of nations, and the moral order inherent in human history testify to God's sovereign rule and moral order.

2.2.3 Revelation through the Inner Moral Law

Every human being has an innate sense of right and wrong, which reflects the moral character of God. This is often referred to as the moral law or conscience. Romans 2:14-15 explains, "Indeed, when Gentiles, who do not have the law, do by nature things required by the law, they are a law for themselves, even though they do not have the law. They show that the requirements of the law are written on their hearts, their consciences also bearing witness, and their thoughts sometimes accusing them and at other times even defending them."

The inner moral law acts as a witness to God's righteous standards and moral nature, pointing individuals to their need for a relationship with Him.

2.3 Special Revelation

Special revelation refers to God's specific and direct communication to humanity, primarily through Scripture and the person of Jesus Christ. This form of revelation is "special" because it provides detailed and explicit knowledge of God's nature, will, and plan for salvation, which cannot be discerned through general revelation alone.

2.3.1 Revelation through Scripture

The Bible is the primary source of special revelation. It is considered the inspired, inerrant Word of God, providing a comprehensive account of God's dealings with humanity. 2 Timothy 3:16-17 states, "All Scripture is God-breathed and is useful for teaching, rebuking, correcting and training in righteousness, so that the servant of God may be thoroughly equipped for every good work."

The Bible reveals God's character, His redemptive plan, and His commandments. It contains historical narratives, laws, poetry, prophecy, and teachings that collectively convey God's revelation to His people. The inspiration of Scripture ensures that it is trustworthy and authoritative for faith and practice.

2.3.2 Revelation through Jesus Christ

The ultimate revelation of God is found in the person of Jesus Christ. Hebrews 1:1-3 declares, "In the past God spoke to our ancestors through the prophets at many times and in various ways, but in these last days He has spoken to us by His Son, whom He appointed heir of all things, and through whom also He made the universe. The Son is the radiance of God's glory and the exact representation of His being, sustaining all things by His powerful word."

Jesus Christ, being fully God and fully man, reveals God's nature, will, and love in a unique and definitive way. Through His life, teachings, death, and resurrection, Jesus provides the clearest and most complete revelation of God.

2.3.3 The Role of the Holy Spirit in Revelation

The Holy Spirit plays a crucial role in both the inspiration of Scripture and the illumination of its truths to believers. The Spirit guided the authors of the Bible to write God's message faithfully and continues to help readers understand and apply its teachings. John 16:13 states, "But when He, the Spirit of truth, comes, He will guide you into all the truth. He will not speak on His own; He will speak only what He hears, and He will tell you what is yet to come."

The Holy Spirit opens the minds and hearts of believers, enabling them to grasp the significance of God's revelation and to live according to its truths.

2.4 The Authority and Inerrancy of Scripture

The authority of Scripture means that the Bible is the ultimate standard for faith and practice. Its teachings are binding on believers, and its commands must be obeyed. This authority is rooted in its divine inspiration; since God is the ultimate author of the Bible, it carries His authority.

2.4.1 Inspiration of Scripture

Inspiration refers to the process by which God guided the human authors of the Bible to write His message without error. 2 Peter 1:20-21 explains, "Above all, you must understand that no prophecy of Scripture came about by the prophet's own interpretation of things. For prophecy never had its origin in the human will, but prophets, though human, spoke from God as they were carried along by the Holy Spirit."

This divine guidance ensured that the Scriptures accurately conveyed God's revelation, making them reliable and authoritative.

2.4.2 Inerrancy of Scripture

Inerrancy means that the Bible, in its original manuscripts, is without error in all that it affirms. This includes not only spiritual and theological truths but also historical and scientific statements, insofar as they pertain to God's revelation. Psalm 19:7 declares, "The law of the Lord is perfect, refreshing the soul. The statutes of the Lord are trustworthy, making wise the simple."

The doctrine of inerrancy underscores the trustworthiness of Scripture, affirming that it is a reliable guide for faith and life.

2.5 The Necessity and Sufficiency of Revelation

2.5.1 The Necessity of Revelation

Revelation is necessary because, without it, humanity cannot know God or His will. Natural revelation provides some knowledge of God's existence and attributes, but it is insufficient for understanding His redemptive plan. Special revelation, particularly through Scripture and Jesus Christ, is necessary for knowing how to be reconciled to God and how to live in accordance with His will.

2.5.2 The Sufficiency of Revelation

The sufficiency of revelation means that the Bible contains all the information necessary for salvation and for living a godly life. 2 Timothy 3:15-17 highlights this sufficiency: "From infancy you have known the Holy Scriptures, which are able to make you wise for salvation through faith in Christ Jesus. All Scripture is God-breathed and is useful for teaching, rebuking, correcting and training in righteousness, so that the servant of God may be thoroughly equipped for every good work."

Scripture provides all the guidance needed for faith and practice, making additional revelations or traditions unnecessary for these purposes.

2.6 Conclusion

The doctrine of revelation is foundational to the Christian faith. It explains how God communicates with humanity, providing the basis for all other theological understanding. Through general revelation, God makes Himself known to all people, revealing His power, wisdom, and moral law. Through special revelation, God discloses specific truths about His nature, will, and redemptive plan, primarily through Scripture and Jesus Christ.

Understanding the nature, authority, and sufficiency of revelation helps believers to trust and apply God's Word in their lives. It ensures that their faith is grounded in the reliable and authoritative self-disclosure of God, leading them to a deeper knowledge of Him and a more faithful walk in His ways. As we continue to explore systematic theology, the truths revealed through God's revelation will form the foundation for our study and understanding of all other doctrines.

2.3 Inspiration and Inerrancy of Scripture

The doctrine of inspiration asserts that the Bible is God-breathed (2 Timothy 3:16). Inerrancy means that Scripture, in its original manuscripts, is without error in all that it affirms. These doctrines underscore the reliability and authority of the Bible, making it the ultimate standard for faith and practice. Understanding inspiration and inerrancy is crucial for appreciating the unique nature of the Bible and its role in conveying divine truth.

2.3.1 The Nature of Biblical Inspiration

Biblical inspiration refers to the process by which God influenced and guided the human authors of the Bible to write His message. This divine influence ensured that their writings were an accurate and authoritative revelation of His will. The concept of inspiration is rooted in the belief that while human authors physically penned the Scriptures, the ultimate source of the content is God Himself.

2.3.1.1 Plenary Verbal Inspiration

Plenary verbal inspiration is the view that every word of the Bible is inspired by God. "Plenary" means that all parts of the Bible are equally inspired, while "verbal" indicates that the very words themselves, not just the ideas or concepts, are God-breathed. This view is supported by passages like Matthew 5:18, where Jesus states, "For truly I tell you, until heaven and earth disappear, not the smallest letter, not the least stroke of a pen, will by any means disappear from the Law until everything is accomplished."

2.3.1.2 The Human Element in Inspiration

While God is the ultimate author of Scripture, He used human writers with their own styles, personalities, and cultural contexts. This dual authorship means that the Bible is both fully divine and fully human. The human authors wrote from their own perspectives and experiences, yet the Holy Spirit ensured that what they wrote was precisely what God intended to communicate.

2.3.2 The Scope of Inerrancy

Inerrancy means that the Bible, in its original manuscripts, is without error in all that it affirms. This doctrine is essential for maintaining the trustworthiness of Scripture. If the Bible contains errors, its authority and reliability would be undermined.

2.3.2.1 Inerrancy and Original Manuscripts

Inerrancy applies to the original manuscripts (autographs) of the Bible, not to the copies or translations. While the original manuscripts are no longer extant, the vast number of existing copies and the science of textual criticism provide confidence that the current biblical text is a faithful representation of the originals.

2.3.2.2 Inerrancy and Truthfulness

Inerrancy means that the Bible is true in all it affirms, whether it speaks on matters of faith, history, science, or ethics. It does not mean that the Bible uses scientific or historical precision by modern standards, but that what it intends to teach is wholly true and reliable. For instance, when the Bible speaks phenomenologically (describing phenomena as they appear, such as the sun "rising"), it is not making a scientific statement but communicating in a way that is understandable and accurate in context.

2.3.3 Challenges to Inerrancy

The doctrine of inerrancy has faced various challenges, both historically and in contemporary times. Addressing these challenges is important for defending the integrity and reliability of Scripture.

2.3.3.1 Alleged Contradictions and Errors

Critics often point to alleged contradictions and errors in the Bible as evidence against inerrancy. However, many of these alleged discrepancies can be resolved through careful exegesis, understanding the context, and recognizing the literary genres used in Scripture. For example, differences in the Gospel accounts of the same event can often be harmonized by recognizing that each author may emphasize different details for theological purposes.

2.3.3.2 Historical and Scientific Criticisms

Some critics argue that the Bible contains historical or scientific inaccuracies. However, inerrancy holds that when properly interpreted, the Bible is true in what it affirms. Historical and archaeological discoveries have often confirmed biblical accounts and apparent scientific errors usually stem from misinterpretations of either the scientific data or the biblical text.

2.3.3.3 Modern Theological Perspectives

In modern theology, some have suggested a limited inerrancy, proposing that the Bible is inerrant in matters of faith and practice but not necessarily in historical or scientific details. This view, however, undermines the total trustworthiness of Scripture and is not consistent with the Bible's own claims about its complete reliability.

2.3.4 The Implications of Inspiration and Inerrancy

Understanding and affirming the doctrines of inspiration and inerrancy has significant implications for how Christians view and use the Bible.

2.3.4.1 Authority of Scripture

Since the Bible is inspired and inerrant, it carries the full authority of God. This means that its teachings are binding on believers, and its commands must be obeyed. The authority of Scripture is foundational for all Christian doctrine and practice.

2.3.4.2 Interpretation of Scripture

Believers must approach the Bible with reverence and a commitment to accurately interpret its message. Hermeneutics, the science of biblical interpretation, involves understanding the text's original meaning and applying it to contemporary contexts. The recognition of Scripture's inerrancy guides interpreters to seek the true meaning of the text without assuming errors or inconsistencies.

2.3.4.3 Trust in God's Word

The doctrine of inerrancy provides believers with confidence in the trustworthiness of God's Word. It assures them that the Bible is a reliable guide for faith and life, capable of leading them into all truth. This trust fosters a deep commitment to studying, meditating on, and living out the teachings of Scripture.

2.3.5 The Witness of the Church to Inspiration and Inerrancy

Throughout history, the church has consistently affirmed the inspiration and inerrancy of Scripture. This witness provides a strong foundation for contemporary believers to hold these doctrines with confidence.

2.3.5.1 Early Church Fathers

The early church fathers, such as Augustine and Athanasius, affirmed the divine inspiration and trustworthiness of Scripture. Augustine famously said, "I have learned to yield this respect and honor only to the canonical books of Scripture: of these alone do I most firmly believe that the authors were completely free from error."

2.3.5.2 Reformation and Post-Reformation Confessions

The Reformers, including Martin Luther and John Calvin, strongly upheld the authority and inerrancy of Scripture. The Westminster Confession of Faith (1646) and other Reformation-era confessions explicitly state that the Bible is infallible and the final authority for faith and practice.

2.3.5.3 Modern Evangelical Affirmations

Modern evangelicalism continues to uphold the doctrines of inspiration and inerrancy. The Chicago Statement on Biblical Inerrancy (1978) is a significant contemporary affirmation, declaring that Scripture is "without error or fault in all its teaching."

2.4 Conclusion

The doctrines of inspiration and inerrancy are foundational for understanding the nature and authority of the Bible. They affirm that Scripture is God-breathed and without error, providing a reliable and authoritative guide for faith and practice. By recognizing the divine inspiration and inerrancy of the Bible, believers can trust in its teachings, confidently interpret its message, and faithfully live out its commands. As we continue to explore systematic theology, these doctrines will serve as the bedrock upon which our understanding of God's revelation and His will is built.

THE DOCTRINE OF GOD

3.1 The Nature of God

The nature of God encompasses His essence and attributes, providing a foundational understanding of who God is and how He relates to His creation. These attributes are central to the Christian understanding of God, and they reveal His greatness and perfection. In this chapter, we will explore the key attributes of God, understanding their implications for our faith and practice.

3.1.1 God as Spirit

God is a spirit, which means that He is immaterial and invisible. This characteristic is fundamental to understanding His nature. John 4:24 states, "God is spirit, and His worshipers must worship in the Spirit and in truth." As a spirit, God is not confined to physical form or limitations, transcending the material universe. His spirituality implies that He is not subject to the physical constraints of time and space, and He can be present everywhere at all times.

This attribute emphasizes the need for spiritual worship and connection with God. It calls believers to recognize that true worship transcends physical rituals and is rooted in the spiritual reality of God's nature.

3.1.2 God as Infinite

God's infinitude refers to His boundlessness and immeasurability. He is not limited by anything outside of Himself and exists beyond all spatial and temporal boundaries. Psalm 147:5 declares, "Great is our Lord and mighty in power; His understanding has no limit." This infinite nature means that God's presence, knowledge, and power are limitless.

God's infinitude assures believers of His ability to be fully present and active in all situations, regardless of their scope or complexity. It underscores the limitless resources available to God in fulfilling His purposes and sustaining His creation.

3.1.3 God as Eternal

God's eternality means that He exists without beginning or end. He transcends time, existing in an eternal present. Psalm 90:2 states, "Before the mountains were born or you brought forth the whole world, from everlasting to everlasting you are God." Unlike created beings, who have a definite beginning and end, God is timeless.

This attribute assures believers that God's purposes and promises are unwavering and eternal. His perspective encompasses all of history, and His plans are not thwarted by temporal limitations. Believers can trust in God's eternal nature, knowing that He remains constant and faithful throughout all ages.

3.1.4 God as Unchangeable

God's immutability means that He does not change in His being, attributes, or purposes. Malachi 3:6 affirms, "I the Lord do not change. So you, the descendants of Jacob, are not destroyed." This unchangeable nature ensures that God's character and promises remain constant and reliable.

God's immutability provides a foundation for trust and stability in the believer's life. In a world of constant change and uncertainty, the unchanging nature of God is a source of comfort and assurance. His promises are dependable, and His character is consistent.

3.1.5 God as All-Wise

God's wisdom means that He has perfect knowledge and understanding, and He always acts according to His perfect will. Romans 11:33 exclaims, "Oh, the depth of the riches of the wisdom and knowledge of God! How unsearchable His judgments, and His paths beyond tracing out!" God's wisdom is evident in creation, providence, and redemption, revealing His ability to bring about the best possible outcomes.

Believers can trust in God's wisdom, knowing that His plans and purposes are ultimately for their good and His glory. This attribute calls for humility and reliance on God's guidance, recognizing that His understanding far surpasses human insight.

3.1.6 God as All-Powerful

God's omnipotence means that He possesses all power and is able to do all that He will. Jeremiah 32:17 declares, "Ah, Sovereign Lord, you have made the heavens and the earth by your great power and outstretched arm. Nothing is too hard for you." God's power is manifest in creation, sustaining the universe, and in the miraculous works throughout history.

God's omnipotence reassures believers of His ability to accomplish His purposes and to intervene in their lives. It encourages faith and dependence on God's power rather than human strength. His omnipotence is a source of hope and confidence in the face of challenges and obstacles.

3.1.7 God as Holy

God's holiness signifies His absolute purity, moral perfection, and separation from sin. Isaiah 6:3 proclaims, "Holy, holy, holy is the Lord Almighty; the whole earth is full of His glory." God's holiness is a defining attribute that sets Him apart from all creation and establishes the standard for moral righteousness.

The holiness of God calls believers to a life of holiness and reverence. It inspires awe and worship, recognizing the majesty and purity of God. Believers are called to reflect God's holiness in their conduct, pursuing a life that is set apart for His purposes.

3.1.8 God as Just

God's justice means that He is perfectly righteous and fair in all His dealings. Deuteronomy 32:4 affirms, "He is the Rock, His works are perfect, and all His ways are just. A faithful God who does no wrong, upright and just is He." God's justice ensures that He upholds moral order and punishes sin while rewarding righteousness.

God's justice is a source of comfort for those who seek righteousness and a warning for those who persist in sin. It assures believers that God will ultimately right all wrongs and bring about justice for the oppressed. God's justice also highlights the need for His grace, as all have sinned and fallen short of His standards.

3.1.9 God as Good

God's goodness encompasses His kindness, benevolence, and love towards His creation. Psalm 34:8 invites, "Taste and see that the Lord is good; blessed is the one who takes refuge in Him." God's goodness is evident in His provision, care, and acts of redemption.

The goodness of God assures believers of His loving care and provision. It inspires gratitude and trust, knowing that God's intentions towards His creation are always good. His goodness motivates believers to reflect His kindness and love in their interactions with others.

3.1.10 God as Truth

God's truthfulness means that He is the ultimate source of all truth, and He is faithful to His promises. Numbers 23:19 declares, "God is not human, that He should lie, not a human being, that He should change His mind. Does He speak and then not act? Does He promise and not fulfill?" God's truth is the foundation of all reality and certainty.

Believers can trust in God's Word, knowing that it is reliable and true. God's truthfulness provides a foundation for faith and a guide for living. It calls believers to uphold truth and integrity in their own lives, reflecting the character of God.

3.1.11 The Unity and Diversity of God's Attributes

While each attribute of God reveals different aspects of His nature, they are not separate or conflicting. God's attributes are perfectly unified and harmonious, each attribute enhancing and complementing the others. For example, God's justice does not contradict His mercy; rather, His mercy is just, and His justice is merciful.

This unity and diversity in God's attributes provide a holistic understanding of His nature. Believers are called to embrace the fullness of God's character, recognizing that each attribute reveals His glory and perfection.

3.1.12 Implications for Worship and Life

Understanding the nature of God has profound implications for worship and daily living. Recognizing God's attributes leads to a deeper reverence and awe in worship. It inspires trust, obedience, and devotion, knowing that God is infinitely worthy of our love and service.

In daily life, the attributes of God provide guidance and assurance. Believers are called to imitate God's holiness, reflect His goodness, rely on His wisdom, and trust in His power. The knowledge of God's unchanging nature and faithfulness provides stability and hope in all circumstances.

3.1.13 Conclusion

The nature of God is foundational to the Christian faith, revealing who God is and how He relates to His creation. Each attribute of God highlights His greatness, perfection, and worthiness of worship. By understanding and reflecting on these attributes, believers can grow in their knowledge of God, deepen their faith, and live lives that honor and glorify Him. As we continue our study of systematic theology, the nature of God will serve as the cornerstone for understanding His works and purposes in the world.

3.2 The Trinity

The doctrine of the Trinity is central to the Christian faith, affirming that God exists as three persons—Father, Son, and Holy Spirit—in one essence. This profound mystery is foundational for understanding God's nature and His relationship with humanity. In this chapter, we will explore the biblical basis for the Trinity, the theological formulation of this doctrine, and its implications for Christian life and worship.

3.2.1 Biblical Basis for the Trinity

The doctrine of the Trinity, while not explicitly named in Scripture, is derived from the cumulative witness of the Bible. Both the Old and New Testaments provide evidence for the triune nature of God.

3.2.1.1 Old Testament Foundations

The Old Testament emphasizes the oneness of God. Deuteronomy 6:4 declares, "Hear, O Israel: The Lord our God, the Lord is one." This foundational statement, known as the Shema, affirms the monotheistic belief central to Judaism and Christianity. However, the Old Testament also contains hints of plurality within the Godhead.

In Genesis 1:26, God says, "Let us make mankind in our image, in our likeness." The plural pronouns suggest a complexity in God's nature. Additionally, passages like Isaiah 48:16 and Isaiah 61:1 include references that Christians interpret as pointing to the distinct persons within the Godhead.

3.2.1.2 New Testament Revelation

The New Testament provides a clearer revelation of the Trinity. The baptism of Jesus in Matthew 3:16-17 reveals all three persons of the Trinity: "As soon as Jesus was baptized, He went up out of the water. At that moment heaven was opened, and He saw the Spirit of God descending like a dove and alighting on Him. And a voice from heaven said, 'This is my Son, whom I love; with Him I am well pleased.'" Here, the Father speaks from heaven, the Son is baptized, and the Spirit descends.

The Great Commission in Matthew 28:19 further affirms the Trinitarian understanding: "Therefore go and make disciples of all nations, baptizing them in the name of the Father and of the Son and of the Holy Spirit." This passage presents the three persons of the Trinity in a unified formula for baptism.

John 14-16 contains extensive teaching by Jesus about the relationship between the Father, Son, and Holy Spirit. Jesus speaks of His unity with the Father (John 14:9-11) and promises the coming of the Holy Spirit, who proceeds from the Father and testifies about the Son (John 15:26).

3.2.2 Theological Formulation of the Trinity

The early church wrestled with the biblical data to formulate a coherent doctrine of the Trinity. This process involved addressing heresies and clarifying the relationship between the Father, Son, and Holy Spirit.

3.2.2.1 Early Church Councils

The Council of Nicaea (325 AD) and the Council of Constantinople (381 AD) were pivotal in the development of Trinitarian doctrine. The Nicene Creed, formulated at these councils, affirmed the full divinity of the Son, stating that He is "of one substance with the Father." The Constantinopolitan Creed expanded this to include the Holy Spirit, declaring that He "proceeds from the Father" and is "worshiped and glorified with the Father and the Son."

3.2.2.2 Key Terminology

To articulate the doctrine of the Trinity, the church developed precise terminology. The term "essence" (Greek: ousia) refers to the single divine nature shared by the Father, Son, and Holy Spirit. The term "person" (Greek: hypostasis) distinguishes the three distinct persons within the Godhead. This language helps to maintain the unity and diversity of God's nature.

3.2.2.3 Trinitarian Heresies

Throughout history, various heresies have challenged the doctrine of the Trinity. Modalism (or Sabellianism) denied the distinction between the persons of the Trinity, viewing them as different modes or manifestations of one God. Arianism denied the full divinity of the Son, claiming that He was a created being. The church's response to these heresies solidified orthodox Trinitarian doctrine, emphasizing both the unity of essence and the distinction of persons.

3.2.3 Implications of the Trinity

The doctrine of the Trinity has profound implications for Christian theology, worship, and life. It shapes our understanding of God, informs our worship practices, and guides our relationships with others.

3.2.3.1 Understanding God

The Trinity reveals that God is inherently relational. The eternal relationship between the Father, Son, and Holy

Spirit reflects the perfect unity and love within the Godhead. This relational nature of God emphasizes that love and community are at the heart of the divine being.

3.2.3.2 Worship

Trinitarian worship acknowledges and honors each person of the Trinity. Christians pray to the Father, through the Son, in the power of the Holy Spirit. The doxologies and hymns of the church often reflect this Trinitarian structure, giving glory to the Father, Son, and Holy Spirit.

3.2.3.3 Salvation

The Trinity is central to the Christian understanding of salvation. The Father's plan of redemption is accomplished through the Son and applied by the Holy Spirit. Ephesians 1:3-14 beautifully illustrates this Trinitarian work: the Father chooses and predestines, the Son redeems through His blood, and the Spirit seals and guarantees our inheritance.

3.2.3.4 Christian Community

The relational nature of the Trinity serves as a model for the Christian community. Just as the Father, Son, and Holy Spirit exist in perfect unity and mutual love, believers are called to live in loving relationships with one another. Jesus prayed for this unity among His followers in John 17:21, "that all of them may be one, Father, just as you are in me and I am in you."

3.2.4 Practical Application

The doctrine of the Trinity is not merely a theological concept; it has practical implications for daily Christian living.

3.2.4.1 Prayer Life

Understanding the Trinity enriches our prayer life. We approach the Father in the name of the Son and through the guidance and power of the Holy Spirit. This Trinitarian approach to prayer helps us to recognize the distinct roles of each person in our communion with God.

3.2.4.2 Worship Practices

Trinitarian doctrine shapes the liturgy and worship practices of the church. Many Christian traditions begin and end their worship services with Trinitarian formulas, invoking the blessing of the Father, Son, and Holy Spirit. This reinforces the centrality of the Trinity in Christian worship.

3.2.4.3 Relationships

The relational aspect of the Trinity serves as a model for our relationships. Just as the Trinity exemplifies perfect love, mutual submission, and unity, Christians are called to embody these qualities in their interactions with others. This includes fostering unity within the church, promoting reconciliation, and practicing self-giving love.

3.2.4.4 Mission and Evangelism

The Great Commission (Matthew 28:19-20) is inherently Trinitarian, commanding believers to baptize in the name of the Father, Son, and Holy Spirit. Understanding the Trinity shapes our mission, as we are sent by the Father, in the authority of the Son, and empowered by the Holy Spirit to make disciples of all nations.

3.2.5 Common Misunderstandings

Despite its centrality, the doctrine of the Trinity is often misunderstood. Clarifying common misconceptions helps to maintain the integrity of this foundational belief.

3.2.5.1 Tritheism

Tritheism is the belief that the Father, Son, and Holy Spirit are three separate gods. This view contradicts the biblical teaching of one God in three persons. The doctrine of the Trinity emphasizes that there is only one divine essence shared by three distinct persons.

3.2.5.2 Modalism

Modalism, or Sabellianism, teaches that God is one person who manifests Himself in three different modes or forms. This denies the distinct personhood of the Father, Son, and Holy Spirit. The biblical witness affirms the distinct and eternal relationships within the Godhead.

3.2.5.3 Subordinationism

Subordinationism suggests that the Son and the Holy Spirit are subordinate in essence to the Father. While the Son and the Spirit willingly submit to the Father's will in their roles, they are co-equal and co-eternal in their essence and divinity. The Nicene Creed affirms that the Son is "of one substance with the Father."

3.2.6 Conclusion

The doctrine of the Trinity is a profound and essential aspect of the Christian faith. It reveals the relational nature of God and provides a framework for understanding His work in creation, redemption, and sanctification. The biblical basis, historical development, and theological articulation of the Trinity underscore its importance for Christian belief and practice.

Understanding the Trinity enhances our worship, deepens our communion with God, and shapes our relationships within the body of Christ. As we continue to explore systematic theology, the doctrine of the Trinity will serve as a guiding principle, reflecting the unity and diversity of the God we worship and serve.

3.3 The Attributes of God

The attributes of God are essential for understanding His nature and how He interacts with His creation. These attributes can be categorized into communicable and incommunicable attributes. Communicable attributes are those that can be found to some extent in humans, such as love and justice. Incommunicable attributes are unique to God, such as omnipresence and immutability. By studying these attributes, we gain a deeper appreciation of God's character and His relationship with us.

3.3.1 Communicable Attributes

Communicable attributes are those aspects of God's character that He shares, to a degree, with humanity. These attributes reflect how God interacts with His creation and how He expects His creatures to reflect His character.

3.3.1.1 Love

God's love is an essential part of His nature. 1 John 4:8 declares, "Whoever does not love does not know God, because God is love." God's love is selfless, sacrificial, and unconditional. It is most profoundly demonstrated in the sending of His Son, Jesus Christ, to die for humanity's sins (John 3:16).

Believers are called to reflect God's love in their interactions with others. This means loving not only those who love us but also those who may be difficult to love. Jesus taught that love is the greatest commandment, encompassing love for God and love for neighbor (Matthew 22:37-39).

3.3.1.2 Justice

God's justice means that He is fair and righteous in all His dealings. Deuteronomy 32:4 states, "He is the Rock, His works are perfect, and all His ways are just. A faithful God who does no wrong, upright and just is He." God's justice ensures that He upholds moral order and that sin is punished.

Human justice reflects God's justice through the establishment of laws and the pursuit of fairness. Christians are called to act justly, love mercy, and walk humbly with God (Micah 6:8). This involves standing up for the oppressed and advocating for righteousness in all areas of life.

3.3.1.3 Mercy

God's mercy is His compassionate treatment of those in distress, sparing them from the punishment they deserve. Lamentations 3:22-23 reminds us, "Because of the Lord's great love we are not consumed, for His compassions never fail. They are new every morning; great is your faithfulness."

Believers are called to be merciful, as their heavenly Father is merciful (Luke 6:36). This means showing compassion and forgiveness to others, recognizing that we have received mercy from God.

3.3.1.4 Holiness

God's holiness signifies His absolute purity and moral perfection. Isaiah 6:3 describes the seraphim calling out, "Holy, holy, holy is the Lord Almighty; the whole earth is full of His glory." God's holiness sets Him apart from all creation and establishes the standard for moral righteousness.

Christians are called to be holy as God is holy (1 Peter 1:16). This involves living a life set apart for God's purposes, avoiding sin, and pursuing righteousness.

3.3.1.5 Faithfulness

God's faithfulness means that He is reliable and true to His promises. Deuteronomy 7:9 says, "Know therefore that the Lord your God is God; He is the faithful God, keeping His covenant of love to a thousand generations of those who love Him and keep His commandments."

Believers are encouraged to be faithful in their relationship with God and in their commitments to others. Faithfulness involves trustworthiness, reliability, and steadfastness.

3.3.1.6 Patience

God's patience, or longsuffering, means that He is slow to anger and patient with humanity's shortcomings. 2 Peter 3:9 explains, "The Lord is not slow in keeping His promise, as some understand slowness. Instead, He is patient with you, not wanting anyone to perish, but everyone to come to repentance."

Christians are called to exhibit patience in their interactions with others, bearing with one another in love

(Ephesians 4:2). Patience involves enduring difficulties without complaint and waiting on God's timing.

3.3.1.7 Goodness

God's goodness encompasses His kindness, benevolence, and generosity. Psalm 34:8 invites us to "taste and see that the Lord is good; blessed is the one who takes refuge in Him." God's goodness is evident in His provision, care, and acts of redemption.

Believers are called to reflect God's goodness by doing good to others, showing kindness, and being generous. This includes acts of service, charity, and promoting the well-being of others.

3.3.2 Incommunicable Attributes

Incommunicable attributes are those aspects of God's character that are unique to Him and not shared with humanity. These attributes highlight God's transcendence and greatness.

3.3.2.1 Omnipresence

God's omnipresence means that He is present everywhere at all times. Psalm 139:7-10 illustrates this truth: "Where can I go from your Spirit? Where can I flee from your presence? If I go up to the heavens, you are there; if I make my bed in the depths, you are there."

God's omnipresence assures believers that He is always with them, no matter where they are or what they are going through. It provides comfort and confidence in His continual presence and care.

3.3.2.2 Omniscience

God's omniscience means that He knows everything, including all past, present, and future events. Hebrews 4:13 states, "Nothing in all creation is hidden from God's sight. Everything is uncovered and laid bare before the eyes of Him to whom we must give account."

God's omniscience assures believers that He understands their situations fully and knows what is best for them. It encourages trust in His wisdom and guidance.

3.3.2.3 Omnipotence

God's omnipotence means that He is all-powerful and able to accomplish anything that is consistent with His nature and will. Jeremiah 32:17 proclaims, "Ah, Sovereign Lord, you have made the heavens and the earth by your great power and outstretched arm. Nothing is too hard for you."

God's omnipotence reassures believers of His ability to intervene in their lives and to fulfill His promises. It inspires faith and confidence in His mighty power.

3.3.2.4 Immutability

God's immutability means that He does not change in His being, attributes, or purposes. Malachi 3:6 affirms, "I the Lord do not change. So you, the descendants of Jacob, are not destroyed."

God's immutability provides stability and assurance to believers. It means that His character, promises, and purposes remain constant, regardless of changing circumstances.

3.3.2.5 Eternality

God's eternality means that He exists without beginning or end and is not bound by time. Psalm 90:2 declares, "Before the mountains were born or you brought forth the whole world, from everlasting to everlasting you are God."

God's eternality assures believers that He is sovereign over time and history. It provides a perspective of His eternal purposes and the hope of eternal life with Him.

3.3.2.6 Self-Existence

God's self-existence, or aseity, means that He exists by Himself and is not dependent on anything or anyone else for His existence. Exodus 3:14 reveals this truth when God declares, "I AM WHO I AM."

God's self-existence highlights His independence and sufficiency. It assures believers that He is the ultimate source of all life and being.

3.3.3 Implications of God's Attributes

Understanding the attributes of God has significant implications for faith and life.

3.3.3.1 Worship

Recognizing God's attributes leads to a deeper and more reverent worship. Acknowledging His holiness, power, and love inspires awe, gratitude, and adoration. Worship becomes a response to the revelation of who God is.

3.3.3.2 Trust

God's attributes provide a solid foundation for trust. Knowing that God is omniscient, omnipotent, and unchanging assures believers that He is fully capable and faithful to fulfill His promises. Trust in God grows as we understand His character more deeply.

3.3.3.3 Ethical Living

God's communicable attributes, such as love, justice, and mercy, provide a model for ethical living. Believers are called to reflect God's character in their interactions with others, promoting righteousness, compassion, and integrity.

3.3.3.4 Assurance and Comfort

God's incommunicable attributes, such as omnipresence and immutability, provide assurance and comfort. Believers can rest in the knowledge that God is always with them, never changes, and is sovereign over all circumstances.

3.3.3.5 Evangelism and Mission

Understanding God's attributes fuels evangelism and mission. Recognizing His love and desire for all people to know Him motivates believers to share the gospel. God's power and wisdom assure them of His ability to work through their efforts to accomplish His purposes.

3.3.4 Conclusion

The attributes of God reveal the richness and depth of His character. Communicable attributes like love, justice, and mercy reflect how God interacts with His creation and how He calls us to live. Incommunicable attributes like omnipresence, omnipotence, and immutability highlight God's transcendence and greatness. By studying and understanding these attributes, believers can grow in their knowledge

of God, deepen their worship, and live lives that reflect His character. As we continue to explore systematic theology, the attributes of God will provide a framework for understanding His actions and purposes in the world.

3.4 The Works of God

The works of God reveal His power, wisdom, and love. They encompass creation, providence, and redemption, showcasing His interaction with the world and His plan for humanity. Understanding these works helps believers appreciate the breadth of God's activity and His continuous involvement in the universe.

3.4.1 Creation

Creation is the foundational work of God, demonstrating His sovereignty and creative power. The Bible opens with the declaration of God's creative act: "In the beginning, God created the heavens and the earth" (Genesis 1:1). This act of creation reveals several key aspects of God's nature and His relationship with the world.

3.4.1.1 The Act of Creation

God created everything ex nihilo, or "out of nothing." Hebrews 11:3 states, "By faith we understand that the universe was formed at God's command, so that what is seen was not made out of what was visible." This emphasizes God's omnipotence and the fact that all things owe their existence to Him.

3.4.1.2 The Goodness of Creation

God declared His creation "very good" (Genesis 1:31). This pronouncement highlights the inherent goodness and orderliness of the created world. Creation reflects God's character, displaying His beauty, wisdom, and purpose.

3.4.1.3 The Purpose of Creation

Creation serves to glorify God. Psalm 19:1 proclaims, "The heavens declare the glory of God; the skies proclaim the work of His hands." Humanity, as part of creation, is made in God's image (Genesis 1:27) and is tasked with stewarding and ruling over the earth (Genesis 1:28).

3.4.1.4 The Sustainer of Creation

God not only created the world but also sustains it. Colossians 1:17 affirms, "He is before all things, and in Him all things hold together." This ongoing sustenance underscores God's continual involvement in and care for His creation. He maintains the natural order and provides for all living beings.

3.4.2 Providence

Providence refers to God's ongoing involvement with and governance over creation. It encompasses His preservation, cooperation, and government of all things, ensuring that His purposes are ultimately fulfilled.

3.4.2.1 Preservation

God preserves His creation, maintaining its existence and sustaining life. Acts 17:28 declares, "For in Him we live and move and have our being." This preservation demonstrates God's care and provision for His creation, ensuring its continued existence and functionality.

3.4.2.2 Cooperation

God cooperates with created things, allowing them to act according to their natures while guiding their actions to fulfill His purposes. Proverbs 16:9 states, "In their hearts humans plan their course, but the Lord establishes their steps." This cooperation means that while creatures have genuine agency, their actions are ultimately directed by God.

3.4.2.3 Government

God governs all things, directing the course of history and the actions of individuals and nations. Psalm 103:19 declares, "The Lord has established His throne in heaven, and His kingdom rules over all." God's government ensures that His sovereign will is accomplished, even amidst human freedom and natural processes.

3.4.2.4 The Problem of Evil

Providence also addresses the problem of evil. While God does not cause evil, He permits it and can bring good out of it. Romans 8:28 assures, "And we know that in all things God works for the good of those who love Him, who have been called according to His purpose." This mystery of providence highlights God's sovereignty and wisdom in managing a world where evil exists.

3.4.3 Redemption

Redemption is the work of God in restoring humanity and creation from the effects of sin. This redemptive plan is centered on Jesus Christ and encompasses His incarnation, atoning death, resurrection, and future return.

3.4.3.1 The Need for Redemption

Humanity's fall into sin created a need for redemption. Romans 3:23 states, "For all have sinned and fall short of the glory of God." Sin separates humanity from God and brings about spiritual and physical death. Redemption is necessary to reconcile humanity to God and restore the relationship broken by sin.

3.4.3.2 The Promise of Redemption

The promise of redemption is woven throughout the Old Testament, beginning with the protoevangelium in Genesis 3:15, which foretells the defeat of the serpent by the offspring of the woman. The covenants with Abraham, Moses, and David further develop the promise of a coming Redeemer who will restore Israel and bless the nations.

3.4.3.3 The Person of Redemption: Jesus Christ

Jesus Christ is the central figure in God's redemptive plan. His incarnation—God becoming man—fulfills the promises of the Old Testament. John 1:14 declares, "The Word became flesh and made His dwelling among us. We have seen His glory, the glory of the one and only Son, who came from the Father, full of grace and truth."

3.4.3.4 The Work of Redemption

Jesus' work of redemption includes His perfect life, atoning death, and victorious resurrection. His sinless life fulfilled the righteous requirements of the law. His sacrificial death on the cross paid the penalty for sin, satisfying God's justice and demonstrating His love (Romans 5:8). His resurrection conquered death, securing eternal life for all who believe (1 Corinthians 15:20-22).

3.4.3.5 The Application of Redemption

Redemption is applied to individuals through the work of the Holy Spirit. The Spirit convicts of sin, regenerates hearts, and grants faith in Christ (John 3:5-8; Ephesians 2:8-9). Believers are justified—declared righteous before God—and adopted into His family (Romans 8:15-17). Sanctification, the process of becoming more like Christ, continues throughout the believer's life (Philippians 1:6).

3.4.3.6 The Consummation of Redemption

Redemption will be fully consummated at the return of Christ. Revelation 21:1-4 describes a new heaven and a new earth, where God dwells with His people, and there is no more death, mourning, crying, or pain. This future hope motivates believers to live faithfully, anticipating the day when God's redemptive plan is fully realized.

3.4.4 The Interrelationship of God's Works

Creation, providence, and redemption are interconnected aspects of God's work. Creation sets the stage for God's providential care and redemptive activity. Providence ensures the continuation and governance of creation, making redemption possible within the created order. Redemption restores and fulfills the purposes of creation, ultimately bringing everything into harmony with God's will.

3.4.4.1 Creation and Providence

God's act of creation is followed by His providential care. The same God who spoke the universe into existence continues to sustain and govern it. Understanding this relationship underscores God's continual involvement with His creation, not as a distant deity but as an ever-present sustainer and ruler.

3.4.4.2 Creation and Redemption

Redemption is a re-creation, a restoration of the original goodness of creation marred by sin. Colossians 1:20 states, "and through Him to reconcile to Himself all things, whether things on earth or things in heaven, by making peace through His blood, shed on the cross." Redemption restores the broken relationship between God and humanity and promises a renewed creation.

3.4.4.3 Providence and Redemption

God's providence includes His redemptive plan. Throughout history, God's sovereign governance has directed events toward the fulfillment of His redemptive purposes. Galatians 4:4-5 explains, "But when the set time had fully come, God sent His Son, born of a woman, born under the law, to redeem those under the law, that we might receive adoption to sonship." Providence ensures that God's redemptive plan unfolds according to His will.

3.4.5 Implications for Believers

Understanding the works of God has significant implications for believers' faith and practice.

3.4.5.1 Trust and Dependence

Recognizing God's work in creation, providence, and redemption fosters trust and dependence on Him. Believers can trust God's power and wisdom, knowing that He is in control of all things and is working for their good (Romans 8:28).

3.4.5.2 Worship and Gratitude

The works of God inspire worship and gratitude. Creation's beauty and complexity, God's sustaining care, and the gift of redemption through Christ all call for a response of awe, praise, and thanksgiving. Worship becomes a way of life, acknowledging God's continuous activity and grace.

3.4.5.3 Stewardship and Responsibility

Understanding God's creative and providential work calls believers to stewardship and responsibility. Humanity is tasked with caring for creation and using resources wisely. Believers are also called to participate in God's redemptive work by sharing the gospel and living out their faith in tangible ways.

3.4.5.4 Hope and Perseverance

The promise of redemption's consummation provides hope and perseverance. Believers can endure trials and challenges, confident that God's redemptive plan will be fulfilled. The future hope of a renewed creation motivates believers to live faithfully and anticipate Christ's return.

3.4.6 Conclusion

The works of God in creation, providence, and redemption reveal His power, wisdom, and love.

These works demonstrate His continuous involvement with the world and His sovereign plan for humanity. Understanding these aspects of God's activity deepens faith, inspires worship, and guides ethical living. As we continue to explore systematic theology, the works of God provide a foundation for understanding His purposes and our place in His plan.

CHAPTER 04

THE PERSON OF CHRIST

4.1 The Person of Christ

The doctrine of the person of Christ, or Christology, is fundamental to Christian theology. It explores the identity and nature of Jesus Christ, who is both fully God and fully man. This dual nature, known as the hypostatic union, is crucial for understanding His redemptive work and the significance of His life, death, and resurrection. In this chapter, we will delve into the biblical basis for Christ's divinity and humanity, the historical development of the doctrine, and its theological implications.

4.1.1 The Divinity of Christ

The divinity of Christ is affirmed throughout the New Testament, which presents Jesus as fully God, sharing in the divine nature and attributes. Several key passages highlight this truth.

4.1.1.1 Biblical Evidence

John 1:1, 14 states, "In the beginning was the Word, and the Word was with God, and the Word was God. ... The Word became flesh and made His dwelling among us. We have seen His glory, the glory of the one and only Son, who came from the Father, full of grace and truth." This passage clearly identifies Jesus (the Word) as God and emphasizes His incarnation.

In Colossians 1:15-20, Paul describes Jesus as "the image of the invisible God, the firstborn over all creation. For in Him all things were created: things in heaven and on earth, visible and invisible, whether thrones or powers or rulers or authorities; all things have been created through Him and for Him. He is before all things, and in Him all things hold together." This passage underscores Jesus' preexistence, creative power, and sustaining role in the universe.

Hebrews 1:3 affirms, "The Son is the radiance of God's glory and the exact representation of His being, sustaining all things by His powerful word." This verse highlights Jesus' divine nature and His role in upholding the universe.

4.1.1.2 Divine Titles and Attributes

Jesus is referred to by titles that denote His divinity, such as "Son of God" (Mark 1:1) and "Lord" (Philippians

2:11). He also possesses attributes unique to God, including omnipotence (Matthew 28:18), omniscience (John 16:30), and eternality (Revelation 22:13).

4.1.1.3 Worship and Prayers Directed to Jesus

Jesus receives worship and prayers, which are due only to God. In John 20:28, Thomas addresses the risen Christ as "My Lord and my God!" Additionally, early Christian prayers and hymns, such as those found in Philippians 2:6-11 and Colossians 1:15-20, honor Jesus as divine.

4.1.2 The Humanity of Christ

Equally important to Christian doctrine is the affirmation of Jesus' full humanity. The New Testament provides ample evidence of Jesus' human nature, experiences, and limitations.

4.1.2.1 Biblical Evidence

John 1:14 declares, "The Word became flesh and made His dwelling among us." This verse affirms the incarnation, where the divine Word took on human flesh.

Philippians 2:7-8 states, "Rather, He made Himself nothing by taking the very nature of a servant, being made in human likeness. And being found in appearance as a man, He humbled Himself by becoming obedient to death—even death on a cross!" This passage emphasizes Jesus' humanity and His willingness to suffer and die.

Hebrews 2:14-17 explains, "Since the children have flesh and blood, He too shared in their humanity so that by His death He might break the power of him who holds the power of death—that is, the devil—and free those who all their lives were held in slavery by their fear of death. For this reason, He had to be made like them, fully human in every way, in order that He might become a merciful and faithful high priest in service to God, and that He might make atonement for the sins of the people."

4.1.2.2 Human Experiences and Emotions

Jesus experienced a full range of human emotions and conditions. He felt hunger (Matthew 4:2), thirst (John 19:28), fatigue (John 4:6), sorrow (John 11:35), and joy (Luke 10:21). He also experienced temptation, yet without sin (Hebrews 4:15).

4.1.2.3 Physical Death and Resurrection

Jesus' physical death on the cross and His bodily resurrection are central to His humanity. He truly suffered and died, and His resurrection involved a physical body, as evidenced by His interactions with His disciples (Luke 24:39).

4.1.3 The Hypostatic Union

The hypostatic union is the theological term that describes the union of Christ's divine and human natures in one person. This doctrine is essential for understanding the nature of Christ and His work of redemption.

4.1.3.1 Definition and Importance

The hypostatic union asserts that Jesus Christ is one person with two distinct but inseparable natures: divine and human. This union is without confusion, change, division, or separation. Each nature retains its own attributes, and both natures are fully and perfectly united in the person of Christ.

4.1.3.2 Biblical Foundation

Key biblical passages support the hypostatic union. John 1:1, 14 and Philippians 2:6-11 affirm both Jesus' divinity and humanity. Colossians 2:9 states, "For in Christ all the fullness of the Deity lives in bodily form." These verses emphasize that Jesus is fully God and fully man.

4.1.3.3 Historical Development

The early church grappled with understanding and articulating the hypostatic union. The Council of Chalcedon (451 AD) provided a definitive statement, affirming that Jesus is "one and the same Christ, Son, Lord, Only-begotten, recognized in two natures, without confusion, without change, without division, without separation." This Chalcedonian Definition remains a cornerstone of orthodox Christology.

4.1.3.4 Theological Significance

The hypostatic union is crucial for several reasons:

- Redemption: Only someone who is both fully God and fully man can mediate between God and humanity (1 Timothy 2:5). Jesus' divinity ensures the infinite value of His sacrifice, while His humanity allows Him to represent humanity and bear its sins.

- Revelation: Jesus perfectly reveals God to humanity. As the God-man, He makes the invisible God known in a tangible way (John 1:18).

- Intercession: As fully human, Jesus sympathizes with our weaknesses and intercedes for us as our high priest (Hebrews 4:15-16).

4.1.4 Implications for Believers

The doctrine of the person of Christ has profound implications for believers' faith and life.

4.1.4.1 Assurance of Salvation

Believers can be assured of their salvation because Jesus, as both God and man, has fully accomplished the work of redemption. His divine nature guarantees the efficacy of His sacrifice, and His human nature ensures that He truly represents us.

4.1.4.2 Model for Living

Jesus' life provides a perfect model for Christian living. His humanity shows us how to live in obedience to

God, love others, and endure suffering. Believers are called to follow His example and live as He lived (1 Peter 2:21).

4.1.4.3 Relationship with God

Through Jesus, believers have a direct and personal relationship with God. He is the mediator who reconciles us to the Father and brings us into intimate fellowship with Him (John 14:6).

4.1.4.4 Hope in Suffering

Jesus' full humanity means that He understands our struggles and suffering. He experienced the full range of human emotions and hardships, and He is able to comfort and strengthen us in our trials (Hebrews 2:18).

4.1.5 Common Misunderstandings

Despite its importance, the doctrine of the person of Christ is often misunderstood. Clarifying these misconceptions helps maintain the integrity of Christological teaching.

4.1.5.1 Docetism

Docetism is the belief that Jesus only appeared to be human but was not truly incarnate. This view denies the reality of Jesus' humanity and His suffering. The New Testament, however, clearly affirms that Jesus came in the flesh (1 John 4:2-3).

4.1.5.2 Arianism

Arianism denies the full divinity of Christ, viewing Him as a created being. This heresy was addressed and condemned at the Council of Nicaea (325 AD), which affirmed the full divinity of the Son, co-equal and co-eternal with the Father.

4.1.5.3 Nestorianism

Nestorianism suggests that Jesus had two separate persons—one divine and one human—rather than one person with two natures. This view was rejected at the Council of Ephesus (431 AD), which upheld the unity of Christ's person.

4.1.5.4 Monophysitism

Monophysitism teaches that Jesus had only one nature, either divine or a synthesis of divine and human. The Council of Chalcedon affirmed that Jesus has two distinct natures, fully divine and fully human, in one person.

4.1.6 Conclusion

The doctrine of the person of Christ is foundational to the Christian faith. Jesus Christ is both fully God and fully man, possessing two natures in one person. This hypostatic union is essential for understanding His redemptive work, His revelation of God, and His role as mediator and intercessor. By affirming the divinity and humanity of Christ, believers can appreciate the depth of God's love, the assurance of salvation, and the hope of eternal life. As we continue to explore systematic theology, the person of Christ remains central to our understanding of God's plan for humanity and His ongoing work in the world.

4.2 The Incarnation

The incarnation is one of the most profound and essential doctrines in Christian theology. It refers to the event in which the Son of God took on human flesh, becoming fully human while remaining fully divine. This remarkable event is foundational to the Christian faith, as it demonstrates God's love, fulfills His redemptive plan, and provides a means for human salvation. In this chapter, we will explore the biblical basis for the incarnation, its theological significance, and its implications for believers.

4.2.1 Biblical Basis for the Incarnation

The incarnation is clearly taught in the New Testament. Several key passages provide the foundation for this doctrine, highlighting both its significance and its purpose.

4.2.1.1 The Gospel of John

John 1:1, 14 is one of the most explicit declarations of the incarnation: "In the beginning was the Word, and the Word was with God, and the Word was God... The Word became flesh and made His dwelling among us. We have seen His glory, the glory of the one and only Son, who came from the Father, full of grace and truth." This passage identifies Jesus as the eternal Word (Logos) who became flesh, highlighting both His divinity and humanity.

4.2.1.2 The Epistles of Paul

Paul's writings also emphasize the incarnation. Philippians 2:6-8 states, "Who, being in very nature God, did not consider equality with God something to be used to His own advantage; rather, He made Himself nothing by taking the very nature of a servant, being made in human likeness. And being found in appearance as a man, He humbled Himself by becoming obedient to death—even death on a cross!" This passage underscores Jesus' preexistence, His voluntary humility, and His obedience unto death.

Galatians 4:4-5 further explains, "But when the set time had fully come, God sent His Son, born of a woman, born under the law, to redeem those under the law, that we might receive adoption to sonship." This highlights the purpose of the incarnation in God's redemptive plan.

4.2.1.3 The Synoptic Gospels

The birth narratives in Matthew and Luke provide additional details about the incarnation. Matthew 1:23 quotes Isaiah 7:14, stating, "The virgin will conceive and give birth to a son, and they will call Him Immanuel" (which means "God with us"). Luke 1:35 describes the angel Gabriel's announcement to Mary: "The Holy Spirit will come on you, and the power of the Most High will overshadow you. So the holy one to be born will be called the Son of God."

4.2.2 Theological Significance of the Incarnation

The incarnation has profound theological significance, impacting several key areas of Christian belief and practice.

4.2.2.1 Revelation of God

The incarnation is the ultimate revelation of God to humanity. Jesus, as God incarnate, makes the invisible God known in a tangible and personal way. John 1:18 states, "No one has ever seen God, but the one and only Son, who is Himself God and is in closest relationship with the Father, has made Him known." Through Jesus, we see the character, love, and will of God revealed.

4.2.2.2 Fulfillment of Prophecy

The incarnation fulfills numerous Old Testament prophecies regarding the coming Messiah. Isaiah 9:6 prophesies, "For to us a child is born, to us a son is given, and the government will be on His shoulders. And He will be called Wonderful Counselor, Mighty God, Everlasting Father, Prince of Peace." The birth of Jesus fulfills these messianic expectations, demonstrating God's faithfulness to His promises.

4.2.2.3 Means of Salvation

The incarnation is central to God's redemptive plan. By becoming human, Jesus was able to represent humanity, live a sinless life, and offer Himself as a perfect sacrifice for sin. Hebrews 2:14-17 explains, "Since the children have flesh and blood, He too shared in their humanity so that by His death He might break the power of him who holds the power of death—that is, the devil—and free those who all their lives were held in slavery by their fear of death. For this reason, He had to be made like them, fully human in every way, in order that He might become a merciful and faithful high priest in service to God, and that He might make atonement for the sins of the people."

4.2.2.4 Defeat of Sin and Death

Through His incarnation, Jesus defeated sin and death, providing eternal life for believers. His resurrection is the proof of His victory and the guarantee of our future resurrection. 1 Corinthians 15:21-22 states, "For since death came through a man, the resurrection of the dead comes also through a man. For as in Adam all die, so in Christ all will be made alive."

4.2.3 Implications for Believers

The doctrine of the incarnation has significant implications for how believers understand their faith and live out their Christian lives.

4.2.3.1 Personal Relationship with God

The incarnation makes it possible for believers to have a personal relationship with God. Jesus, as Immanuel ("God with us"), bridges the gap between a holy God and sinful humanity. Through faith in Christ, believers are adopted into God's family and can approach Him with confidence (Ephesians 3:12).

4.2.3.2 Model of Humility and Service

Jesus' incarnation serves as the ultimate example of humility and service. Philippians 2:5-7 exhorts believers to have the same mindset as Christ, "Who, being in very nature God, did not consider equality with God something to be used to His own advantage; rather, He made Himself nothing by taking the very nature of a servant, being made in human likeness." Believers are called to emulate Jesus' selflessness and sacrificial love in their interactions with others.

4.2.3.3 Hope and Comfort

The incarnation provides hope and comfort to believers. Jesus, having experienced human life in all its fullness, understands our struggles and sufferings. Hebrews 4:15-16 assures us, "For we do not have a high priest who is unable to empathize with our weaknesses, but we have one who has been tempted in every way, just as we are—yet He did not sin. Let us then approach God's throne of grace with confidence, so that we may receive mercy and find grace to help us in our time of need."

4.2.3.4 Mission and Evangelism

The incarnation motivates believers to share the gospel. Just as God sent His Son into the world, Jesus sends His followers to proclaim the good news of salvation. John 20:21 records Jesus' commission: "As the Father has sent me, I am sending you." The incarnation underscores the urgency and importance of the missionary task.

4.2.4 Historical and Theological Challenges

Throughout church history, the doctrine of the incarnation has faced various challenges and misunderstandings. Addressing these helps to clarify and reinforce orthodox Christian beliefs.

4.2.4.1 Early Heresies

Several early heresies attempted to undermine the incarnation. Docetism denied that Jesus had a real human body, suggesting that His physical form was an illusion. The church rejected this view, affirming Jesus' true humanity.

Another heresy, Apollinarianism, taught that Jesus had a human body but a divine mind, thereby denying His full humanity. The Council of Constantinople (381 AD) condemned this view, upholding the belief that Jesus is fully human and fully divine.

4.2.4.2 Modern Challenges

In modern times, some theologians question the historical accuracy of the incarnation narratives or reinterpret them symbolically. However, orthodox Christianity maintains the historical reality of the incarnation as essential to the faith.

4.2.4.3 Theological Clarifications

The Council of Chalcedon (451 AD) provided a definitive statement on the incarnation, affirming that Jesus is "truly God and truly man, of a reasonable soul and body; consubstantial with the Father according to the Godhead, and consubstantial with us according to the Manhood; in all things like unto us, without sin." This Chalcedonian Definition remains a cornerstone of Christological orthodoxy.

4.2.5 Conclusion

The incarnation is a central and essential doctrine of the Christian faith. It reveals the depth of God's love, fulfills His redemptive plan, and provides the means for human salvation. Through the incarnation, Jesus, the Son of God, became fully human while remaining fully divine. This mystery of the hypostatic union is foundational for understanding the person and work of Christ.

For believers, the incarnation offers profound implications for their relationship with God, their conduct, and their mission. It provides a model of humility and service, a source of hope and comfort, and a motivation for evangelism. As we continue to explore systematic theology, the incarnation remains a cornerstone for understanding God's interaction with humanity and His ultimate plan for redemption.

4.3 The Work of Christ

The work of Christ is central to the Christian faith, encompassing His atoning death on the cross, His resurrection, and His ascension. Each aspect of Christ's work plays a vital role in the salvation of humanity, revealing the depth of God's love, justice, and power. In this chapter, we will explore these key elements of Christ's work, their biblical basis, theological significance, and practical implications for believers.

4.3.1 The Atoning Death of Christ

The atoning death of Christ is the cornerstone of His redemptive work. Through His sacrifice on the cross, Jesus bore the penalty for sin, satisfied God's justice, and reconciled humanity to God.

4.3.1.1 Biblical Basis

The New Testament consistently emphasizes the significance of Christ's death. Isaiah 53:5-6 prophetically describes the suffering servant who bears the iniquities of humanity: "But He was pierced for our transgressions, He was crushed for our iniquities; the punishment that brought us peace was on Him, and by His wounds, we are healed. We all, like sheep, have gone astray, each of us has turned to our own way; and the Lord has laid on Him the iniquity of us all."

In the Gospels, Jesus repeatedly speaks of His impending death as a necessary part of His mission (Mark 10:45; John 12:27). Paul's epistles further expound on the theological meaning of Christ's death. Romans 3:25-26 states, "God presented Christ as a sacrifice of atonement, through the shedding of His blood—to be received by faith. He did this to demonstrate His righteousness because in His forbearance He had left the sins committed beforehand unpunished—He did it to demonstrate His righteousness at the present time, so as to be just and the one who justifies those who have faith in Jesus."

4.3.1.2 Theological Significance

The atonement involves several key theological concepts:

- Substitution: Jesus took the place of sinners, bearing the punishment they deserved. This substitutionary aspect is highlighted in 2 Corinthians 5:21, "God made Him who had no sin to be sin for us so that in Him we might become the righteousness of God."

- Propitiation: Christ's death appeased the wrath of God against sin. Romans 3:25 uses the term "propitiation" (or "sacrifice of atonement") to describe how Jesus' sacrifice satisfies God's righteous anger.

- Redemption: Jesus' death redeems believers from the bondage of sin. Ephesians 1:7 states, "In Him we have redemption through His blood, the forgiveness of sins, in accordance with the riches of God's grace."

- Reconciliation: Through His death, Jesus reconciles humanity to God, restoring the broken relationship caused by sin. Colossians 1:20 explains, "And through Him to reconcile to Himself all things, whether things on earth or things in heaven, by making peace through His blood, shed on the cross."

4.3.1.3 Practical Implications

The atoning death of Christ has profound implications for believers:

- Forgiveness of Sins: Believers receive full and complete forgiveness of their sins through Jesus' sacrifice. This forgiveness is a gift of grace, received by faith (Ephesians 2:8-9).

- Peace with God: Through Christ's atonement, believers are reconciled to God and enjoy peace with Him (Romans 5:1).

- New Identity: Believers are no longer defined by their sin but by their new identity in Christ. They are adopted into God's family and are heirs of His promises (Romans 8:15-17).

4.3.2 The Resurrection of Christ

The resurrection of Christ is a pivotal event in Christian history. It confirms Jesus' victory over sin and death, validates His divine identity, and provides the basis for the believer's hope of eternal life.

4.3.2.1 Biblical Basis

The New Testament provides numerous accounts of the resurrection. The Gospels record the discovery of the empty tomb and Jesus' appearances to His disciples (Matthew 28; Mark 16; Luke 24; John 20-21). Paul emphasizes the importance of the resurrection in 1 Corinthians 15:3-4, "For what I received I passed on to you as of first importance: that Christ died for our sins according to the Scriptures, that He was buried, that He was raised on the third day according to the Scriptures."

4.3.2.2 Theological Significance

The resurrection has several key theological implications:

- Validation of Jesus' Claims: The resurrection confirms Jesus' identity as the Son of God and validates His teachings. Romans 1:4 declares that Jesus "was declared with power to be the Son of God by His resurrection from the dead."

- Victory Over Death: Jesus' resurrection conquers death, providing the basis for believers' future resurrection. 1 Corinthians 15:54-57 celebrates this victory: "Death has been swallowed up in victory. Where, O death, is your victory? Where, O death, is your sting? ... Thanks be to God! He gives us the victory through our Lord Jesus Christ."

- Foundation for Justification: The resurrection is essential for the believer's justification. Romans 4:25 states, "He was delivered over to death for our sins and was raised to life for our justification."

4.3.2.3 Practical Implications

The resurrection of Christ has significant implications for the believer's life and hope:

- Assurance of Eternal Life: Believers have the assurance of eternal life because of Jesus' resurrection. John 11:25-26 records Jesus' promise: "I am the resurrection and the life. The one who believes in me will live, even though they die; and whoever lives by believing in me will never die."

- Empowerment for Christian Living: The resurrection power of Christ enables believers to live victorious lives. Ephesians 1:19-20 speaks of "His incomparably great power for us who believe. That power is the same as the mighty strength He exerted when He raised Christ from the dead."

- Hope in Suffering: The resurrection provides hope and perspective in the face of suffering and death. Believers are encouraged to persevere, knowing that their future is secure in Christ (1 Peter 1:3-5).

4.3.3 The Ascension of Christ

The ascension of Christ marks the culmination of His earthly ministry and His exaltation to the right hand of the Father. It signifies His ongoing work and intercession for believers.

4.3.3.1 Biblical Basis

The ascension is recorded in Luke 24:50-53 and Acts 1:9-11. Acts 1:9 describes the event: "After He said this, He was taken up before their very eyes, and a cloud hid Him from their sight." The New Testament also frequently refers to Jesus' exalted position at the right hand of God (Ephesians 1:20; Hebrews 1:3).

4.3.3.2 Theological Significance

The ascension has several key theological implications:

- Exaltation and Lordship: The ascension signifies Jesus' exaltation and His authority as Lord. Philippians 2:9-11 declares, "Therefore God exalted Him to the highest place and gave Him the name that is above every name, that at the name of Jesus, every knee should bow, in heaven and on earth and under the earth, and every tongue acknowledge that Jesus Christ is Lord, to the glory of God the Father."

- Intercession: Jesus' ascension marks the beginning of His high priestly intercession for believers. Hebrews 7:25 states, "Therefore He is able to save completely those who come to God through Him because He always lives to intercede for them."

- Preparation of a Place: Jesus ascends to prepare a place for His followers. John 14:2-3 records His promise: "My Father's house has many rooms; if that were not so, would I have told you that I am going there to prepare a place for you? And if I go and prepare a place for you, I will come back and take you to be with me so that you also may be where I am."

4.3.3.3 Practical Implications

The ascension of Christ has practical implications for the believer's faith and practice:

- Confidence in Prayer: Believers can approach God with confidence, knowing that Jesus intercedes on their behalf (Hebrews 4:14-16).

- Empowerment for Mission: The ascension is linked to the sending of the Holy Spirit, who empowers believers for mission. Acts 1:8 records Jesus' promise: "But you will receive power when the Holy Spirit comes on you, and you will be my witnesses in Jerusalem, and in all Judea and Samaria, and to the ends of the earth."

- Hope for Christ's Return: The ascension assures believers of Jesus' return. Acts 1:11 records the angels' message: "This same Jesus, who has been taken from you into heaven, will come back in the same way you have seen Him go into heaven."

4.3.4 Common Misunderstandings

Despite its central importance, the work of Christ is often misunderstood. Addressing these misconceptions helps to preserve the integrity of Christian doctrine.

4.3.4.1 Moral Influence Theory

The moral influence theory

suggests that Christ's death primarily serves as a demonstration of God's love, intended to inspire moral improvement. While it is true that Jesus' sacrifice reveals God's love, this view neglects the substitutionary and propitiatory aspects of the atonement. The New Testament clearly teaches that Jesus' death was a sacrifice for sin, satisfying God's justice and providing redemption.

4.3.4.2 Christus Victor

The Christus Victor theory emphasizes Christ's victory over the powers of sin, death, and Satan. While this is a valid and important aspect of the atonement, it should not be viewed in isolation. The full biblical picture includes the substitutionary nature of Christ's sacrifice and the legal aspects of justification and redemption.

4.3.4.3 Denial of the Resurrection

Some modern interpretations deny the historical reality of the resurrection, viewing it as a metaphor for new life or spiritual renewal. However, the New Testament affirms the bodily resurrection of Jesus as a historical event that is foundational to the Christian faith. Without the resurrection, the apostle Paul argues, the Christian faith is futile (1 Corinthians 15:17).

4.3.5 Conclusion

The work of Christ is the heart of the Christian gospel. His atoning death on the cross, His victorious resurrection, and His exalted ascension are central to God's redemptive plan. Through these acts, Jesus accomplished salvation for humanity, defeating sin and death, reconciling believers to God, and securing eternal life.

Understanding the work of Christ deepens believers' faith, inspires worship, and motivates mission. It provides the foundation for a personal relationship with God, offers hope in the face of suffering and death, and empowers believers to live transformed lives. As we continue to explore systematic theology, the work of Christ remains a central focus, reflecting the depth of God's love and the power of His saving grace.

4.4 The Offices of Christ

The doctrine of the offices of Christ is essential to understanding His multifaceted role in God's redemptive plan. Jesus Christ fulfills three primary offices: prophet, priest, and king. Each office highlights a different aspect of His work and ministry, demonstrating how He perfectly meets the needs of humanity and accomplishes the purposes of God. In this chapter, we will explore the biblical basis, theological significance, and practical implications of Christ's roles as prophet, priest, and king.

4.4.1 Christ as Prophet

As a prophet, Jesus reveals God's truth to humanity. Prophets in the Old Testament were God's spokespeople, delivering His messages to the people. Jesus, the ultimate prophet, perfectly reveals God's will and truth.

4.4.1.1 Biblical Basis

Deuteronomy 18:15-18 foretells the coming of a prophet like Moses: "The Lord your God will raise up for you a prophet like me from among you, from your fellow Israelites. You must listen to Him. ... I will put my words in His mouth, and He will tell them everything I command Him." The New Testament identifies Jesus as this promised prophet (Acts 3:22-23).

In the Gospels, Jesus frequently teaches with authority, revealing God's truth and will. For example, in the Sermon on the Mount (Matthew 5-7), Jesus expounds the deeper meanings of the Law and calls people to a higher standard of righteousness. John 1:18 emphasizes that Jesus has made God known: "No one has ever seen God, but the one and only Son, who is Himself God and is in closest relationship with the Father, has made Him known."

4.4.1.2 Theological Significance

Jesus' role as prophet is significant for several reasons:

- Revelation of God: Jesus reveals the nature and character of God more fully than any previous prophet. He is the "exact representation" of God's being (Hebrews 1:3) and declares the Father's will perfectly.

\- Fulfillment of Prophecy: Jesus fulfills the prophetic tradition, not only by predicting future events but by embodying and actualizing God's redemptive plan.

\- Foundation of Teaching: Jesus' teachings provide the foundation for Christian doctrine and ethical living. His words are authoritative and timeless, guiding believers in truth.

4.4.1.3 Practical Implications

The prophetic office of Christ has practical implications for believers:

\- Guidance and Instruction: Believers look to Jesus' teachings for guidance in their faith and practice. His words provide direction for living a life that honors God.

\- Model of Proclamation: As followers of Christ, believers are called to proclaim His truth to others, sharing the gospel and teaching His commandments (Matthew 28:19-20).

\- Discernment of Truth: Jesus' role as prophet helps believers discern truth from falsehood, grounding their faith in His authoritative teachings.

4.4.2 Christ as Priest

As a priest, Jesus mediates between God and humanity. In the Old Testament, priests offered sacrifices and interceded on behalf of the people. Jesus, the ultimate high priest, offers Himself as the perfect sacrifice and continually intercedes for believers.

4.4.2.1 Biblical Basis

Hebrews 4:14-16 declares, "Therefore since we have a great high priest who has ascended into heaven, Jesus the Son of God, let us hold firmly to the faith we profess. For we do not have a high priest who is unable to empathize with our weaknesses, but we have one who has been tempted in every way, just as we are—yet He did not sin. Let us then approach God's throne of grace with confidence, so that we may receive mercy and find grace to help us in our time of need."

Hebrews 7:24-25 further explains, "but because Jesus lives forever, He has a permanent priesthood. Therefore He is able to save completely those who come to God through Him, because He always lives to intercede for them."

4.4.2.2 Theological Significance

Jesus' role as priest is crucial for several reasons:

- Atonement for Sin: Jesus offers Himself as the perfect and final sacrifice for sin. His death on the cross satisfies God's justice and secures forgiveness for believers (Hebrews 9:12-14).

- Intercession: Jesus continually intercedes for believers, representing them before the Father and ensuring their access to God's grace (Romans 8:34).

- Sympathy and Understanding: As a high priest who has experienced human weakness and temptation, Jesus empathizes with believers and provides comfort and support (Hebrews 4:15).

4.4.2.3 Practical Implications

The priestly office of Christ has practical implications for believers:

- Confidence in Approach: Believers can approach God with confidence, knowing that Jesus intercedes for them and that their sins are forgiven (Hebrews 4:16).

- Assurance of Salvation: Jesus' continual intercession assures believers of their salvation and sustains them in their faith (Hebrews 7:25).

- Call to Holiness: Jesus' sacrifice calls believers to live lives of holiness and gratitude, reflecting the transformative power of His atonement (1 Peter 1:15-16).

4.4.3 Christ as King

As a king, Jesus reigns over all creation. In the Old Testament, kings were anointed to rule and govern God's people. Jesus, the ultimate king, is sovereign over all and establishes His kingdom of justice and peace.

4.4.3.1 Biblical Basis

Psalm 2:6-7 prophesies the coronation of God's anointed king: "I have installed my king on Zion, my holy mountain. I will proclaim the Lord's decree: He said to me, 'You are my son; today I have become your father.'" The New Testament identifies Jesus as this promised king. In Luke 1:32-33, the angel Gabriel announces to Mary, "He will be great and will be called the Son of the Most High. The Lord God will give Him the throne of His father David, and He will reign over Jacob's descendants forever; His kingdom will never end."

In Revelation 19:16, Jesus is described as the King of kings and Lord of lords: "On His robe and on His thigh He has this name written: king of kings and lord of lords."

4.4.3.2 Theological Significance

Jesus' role as king is significant for several reasons:

- Sovereign Authority: Jesus exercises sovereign authority over all creation. He governs the universe and directs history according to God's plan (Ephesians 1:20-22).

- Establishment of the Kingdom: Jesus inaugurates God's kingdom, bringing justice, peace, and righteousness. His reign contrasts with earthly kingdoms and reflects divine values (Matthew 4:17).

- Defeat of Evil: As king, Jesus defeats the powers of sin, death, and Satan. His victory on the cross and His future return establish His ultimate dominion (1 Corinthians 15:24-26).

4.4.3.3 Practical Implications

The kingly office of Christ has practical implications for believers:

- Allegiance and Obedience: Believers are called to submit to Jesus' authority and live in obedience to His commands. His lordship requires wholehearted allegiance (Luke 6:46).

- Participation in the Kingdom: Believers participate in Jesus' kingdom by promoting justice, peace, and righteousness in their communities. They are ambassadors of His reign (2 Corinthians 5:20).

- Hope and Anticipation: The promise of Jesus' return as king provides hope and motivates believers to live faithfully in anticipation of His coming kingdom (Titus 2:13).

4.4.4 The Interrelationship of Christ's Offices

While each office of Christ—prophet, priest, and king—has distinct aspects, they are interrelated and together provide a comprehensive understanding of His work.

4.4.4.1 Unity in Christ

Jesus perfectly fulfills all three offices, demonstrating the unity and completeness of His work. As prophet, He reveals God's truth; as priest, He provides the means of reconciliation; and as king, He exercises sovereign authority.

These roles are not isolated but interconnected, each contributing to the fulfillment of God's redemptive plan.

4.4.4.2 Fulfillment of Old Testament Types

The offices of Christ fulfill the Old Testament types and shadows. Prophets, priests, and kings in the Old Testament prefigure Christ's work. He is the ultimate prophet who reveals God, the perfect priest who mediates between God and humanity, and the eternal king who reigns with justice and peace.

4.4.4.3 Comprehensive Ministry

The combined offices of Christ ensure a comprehensive ministry that addresses all aspects of human need. His prophetic role enlightens, His priestly role reconciles, and His kingly role governs. Together, they provide a complete picture of Jesus' mission and ministry.

4.4.5 Conclusion

The offices of Christ—prophet, priest, and king—are essential for understanding His multifaceted work in God's redemptive plan. As a prophet, Jesus reveals God's truth; as a priest, He intercedes for humanity and provides the means of reconciliation; and as a king, He reigns over all creation with sovereign authority.

Understanding these roles deepens believers' faith, enriches their worship, and guides their conduct. It highlights the comprehensive nature of Jesus' ministry and His sufficiency to meet all human needs. As we continue to

explore systematic theology, the offices of Christ remain central to our understanding of His person and work, reflecting the fullness of His mission to redeem and restore humanity.

CHAPTER 05

THE PERSON OF THE HOLY SPIRIT

5.1 The Person of the Holy Spirit

The doctrine of the Holy Spirit, or pneumatology, is essential to understanding the Christian faith. The Holy Spirit is the third person of the Trinity, fully God, co-equal, and co-eternal with the Father and the Son. Recognizing the personhood of the Holy Spirit is crucial for appreciating His role in the life of believers and the church. In this chapter, we will explore the biblical basis for the Holy Spirit's divinity and personhood, His attributes, and His personal activities.

5.1.1 The Divinity of the Holy Spirit

The divinity of the Holy Spirit is clearly affirmed in the Scriptures. The Holy Spirit possesses the attributes of God and is involved in divine activities, underscoring His full divinity.

5.1.1.1 Biblical Evidence

Several passages in the New Testament explicitly affirm the divinity of the Holy Spirit. Acts 5:3-4 records Peter's confrontation with Ananias: "Then Peter said, 'Ananias, how is it that Satan has so filled your heart that you have lied to the Holy Spirit... You have not lied just to human beings but to God.'" This passage equates lying to the Holy Spirit with lying to God.

In 1 Corinthians 3:16, Paul writes, "Don't you know that you yourselves are God's temple and that God's Spirit dwells in your midst?" Here, the presence of the Holy Spirit within believers is equated with the presence of God.

5.1.1.2 Attributes of Divinity

The Holy Spirit possesses divine attributes that are unique to God:

- Omniscience: The Holy Spirit knows all things. 1 Corinthians 2:10-11 states, "The Spirit searches all things, even the deep things of God. For who knows a person's thoughts except their own spirit within them? In the same way no one knows the thoughts of God except the Spirit of God."

- Omnipresence: The Holy Spirit is present everywhere. Psalm 139:7-8 declares, "Where can I go from your Spirit? Where can I flee from your presence? If I go up to the heavens, you are there; if I make my bed in the depths, you are there."

- Eternality: The Holy Spirit is eternal. Hebrews 9:14 refers to Him as "the eternal Spirit."

5.1.1.3 Involvement in Divine Activities

The Holy Spirit is involved in divine activities such as creation, revelation, and sanctification:

- Creation: The Holy Spirit was active in creation. Genesis 1:2 states, "Now the earth was formless and empty... and the Spirit of God was hovering over the waters."

- Revelation: The Holy Spirit inspired the Scriptures. 2 Peter 1:21 explains, "For prophecy never had its origin in the human will, but prophets, though human, spoke from God as they were carried along by the Holy Spirit."

- Sanctification: The Holy Spirit sanctifies believers. 1 Corinthians 6:11 says, "But you were washed, you were sanctified, you were justified in the name of the Lord Jesus Christ and by the Spirit of our God."

5.1.2 The Personhood of the Holy Spirit

The Holy Spirit is not an impersonal force but a personal being who possesses intellect, emotions, and will. Recognizing the personhood of the Holy Spirit is essential for understanding His active role in the life of believers and the church.

5.1.2.1 Intellect

The Holy Spirit possesses intellect and knowledge. 1 Corinthians 2:10-11, as mentioned earlier, highlights the Spirit's ability to search and know the deep things of God. This attribute underscores the Spirit's capacity for understanding and wisdom.

5.1.2.2 Emotions

The Holy Spirit has emotions and can be grieved. Ephesians 4:30 exhorts believers, "And do not grieve the Holy Spirit of God, with whom you were sealed for the day of redemption." This passage indicates that the Spirit can experience grief, demonstrating His emotional capacity.

5.1.2.3 Will

The Holy Spirit exercises will and makes decisions. 1 Corinthians 12:11 describes the Spirit's distribution of spiritual gifts: "All these are the work of one and the same Spirit, and He distributes them to each one, just as He determines." The Spirit's sovereign will is evident in the allocation of gifts within the church.

5.1.3 Personal Activities of the Holy Spirit

The Holy Spirit engages in activities that reflect His personhood and His involvement in the lives of believers and the church. These activities include speaking, teaching, guiding, and interceding.

5.1.3.1 Speaking

The Holy Spirit speaks to and through believers. Acts 13:2 records the Spirit's directive to the church at Antioch: "While they were worshiping the Lord and fasting, the Holy Spirit said, 'Set apart for me Barnabas and Saul for the work to which I have called them.'" This passage demonstrates the Spirit's active communication with the church.

5.1.3.2 Teaching

The Holy Spirit teaches and reminds believers of Jesus' teachings. John 14:26 promises, "But the Advocate, the Holy Spirit, whom the Father will send in my name, will teach you all things and will remind you of everything I have said to you." The Spirit's role as a teacher ensures that believers grow in their understanding of God's truth.

5.1.3.3 Guiding

The Holy Spirit guides believers into all truth. John 16:13 states, "But when He, the Spirit of truth, comes, He will guide you into all the truth. He will not speak on His own; He will speak only what He hears, and He will tell you what is yet to come." This guidance helps believers navigate their spiritual journey and discern God's will.

5.1.3.4 Interceding

The Holy Spirit intercedes for believers, praying on their behalf. Romans 8:26-27 explains, "In the same way, the Spirit helps us in our weakness. We do not know what we ought to pray for, but the Spirit Himself intercedes for us through wordless groans. And He who searches our hearts knows the mind of the Spirit, because the Spirit intercedes for God's people in accordance with the will of God." The Spirit's intercession aligns believers' prayers with God's will and provides support in times of need.

5.1.4 The Holy Spirit in the Trinity

The Holy Spirit's role within the Trinity emphasizes His co-equality and co-eternality with the Father and the Son. Understanding this relationship is essential for a balanced and comprehensive view of the Trinity.

5.1.4.1 Co-equal and Co-eternal

The Holy Spirit is co-equal and co-eternal with the Father and the Son. The Great Commission in Matthew 28:19 reflects this equality: "Therefore go and make disciples of all nations, baptizing them in the name of the Father and of the Son and of the Holy Spirit." This Trinitarian formula underscores the equal status and divine nature of each person of the Trinity.

5.1.4.2 Procession of the Holy Spirit

The procession of the Holy Spirit refers to His relationship within the Trinity. The Nicene Creed (381 AD) states that the Holy Spirit "proceeds from the Father." The Western Church later added the phrase "and the Son" (Filioque), leading to the understanding that the Spirit proceeds from both the Father and the Son. This concept highlights the unity and interrelationship within the Trinity.

5.1.4.3 Unity and Diversity

The Holy Spirit, along with the Father and the Son, shares the same divine essence while maintaining distinct personal roles. This unity in diversity is central to the Trinitarian understanding and emphasizes the harmonious relationship within the Godhead.

5.1.5 Practical Implications for Believers

Recognizing the personhood and divinity of the Holy Spirit has profound practical implications for the life of believers.

5.1.5.1 Personal Relationship

Believers can cultivate a personal relationship with the Holy Spirit, acknowledging His presence, seeking His guidance, and responding to His leading. This relationship enhances spiritual growth and intimacy with God.

5.1.5.2 Empowerment for Ministry

The Holy Spirit empowers believers for ministry and service. Acts 1:8 promises, "But you will receive power when the Holy Spirit comes on you, and you will be my witnesses in Jerusalem, and in all Judea and Samaria, and to the ends of the earth." The Spirit equips and enables believers to fulfill their mission.

5.1.5.3 Guidance and Comfort

Believers can rely on the Holy Spirit for guidance and comfort. His role as guide and intercessor provides direction and support in times of uncertainty and difficulty. This reliance fosters trust and dependence on God.

5.1.5.4 Holiness and Transformation

The Holy Spirit sanctifies believers, transforming them into the likeness of Christ. Galatians 5:22-23 describes the fruit of the Spirit, which includes love, joy, peace, patience, kindness, goodness, faithfulness, gentleness, and self-control. The Spirit's work produces holiness and character transformation in believers' lives.

5.1.6 Conclusion

The Holy Spirit is the third person of the Trinity, fully God, co-equal, and co-eternal with the Father and the Son. Recognizing His divinity and personhood is essential for understanding His role in the life of believers and the church. The Holy Spirit's attributes and activities demonstrate His active involvement in guiding, teaching, comforting, and transforming believers.

Understanding the person of the Holy Spirit deepens believers' relationship with God, empowers their ministry, and fosters spiritual growth. As we continue to explore systematic theology, the doctrine of the Holy Spirit remains central to our comprehension of God's work and presence in the world.

5.2 The Work of the Holy Spirit

The work of the Holy Spirit is vital to the Christian life, encompassing regeneration, indwelling, sanctification, and empowerment. The Holy Spirit plays a crucial role in bringing believers to faith, sustaining their spiritual growth, and equipping them for service. In this chapter, we will explore these key aspects of the Spirit's work, examining their biblical basis, theological significance, and practical implications.

5.2.1 Regeneration

Regeneration, or the new birth, is the work of the Holy Spirit by which He imparts spiritual life to those who are spiritually dead. This transformative act makes believers new creations in Christ.

5.2.1.1 Biblical Basis

Titus 3:5 explains, "He saved us, not because of righteous things we had done, but because of His mercy. He saved us through the washing of rebirth and renewal by the Holy Spirit." This passage highlights the Spirit's role in the cleansing and renewal associated with salvation.

Jesus' conversation with Nicodemus in John 3:5-6 further underscores the necessity of regeneration: "Jesus answered, 'Very truly I tell you, no one can enter the kingdom of God unless they are born of water and the Spirit. Flesh gives birth to flesh, but the Spirit gives birth to spirit.'" Regeneration is a spiritual rebirth brought about by the Holy Spirit.

5.2.1.2 Theological Significance

Regeneration is essential for entering the kingdom of God and experiencing a relationship with Him. It involves a fundamental transformation of the believer's nature, moving from spiritual death to spiritual life. 2 Corinthians 5:17 affirms, "Therefore, if anyone is in Christ, the new creation has come: The old has gone, the new is here!"

5.2.1.3 Practical Implications

- New Identity: Believers are given a new identity in Christ. They are no longer defined by their past sins but are made new creations, with a new heart and spirit.

- Assurance of Salvation: Regeneration provides assurance of salvation. The inward change wrought by the Spirit confirms the believer's status as a child of God.

- Beginning of Sanctification: Regeneration marks the beginning of the sanctification process, as the Spirit continues to work in the believer's life to produce holiness.

5.2.2 Indwelling

The Holy Spirit indwells believers, taking up residence within them and providing ongoing guidance, assurance, and comfort.

5.2.2.1 Biblical Basis

Romans 8:9 states, "You, however, are not in the realm of the flesh but are in the realm of the Spirit, if indeed the Spirit of God lives in you. And if anyone does not have the Spirit of Christ, they do not belong to Christ." This verse affirms that the indwelling of the Spirit is a mark of genuine Christian identity.

1 Corinthians 6:19-20 further emphasizes, "Do you not know that your bodies are temples of the Holy Spirit, who is in you, whom you have received from God? You are not your own; you were bought at a price. Therefore honor God with your bodies." Believers' bodies are temples of the Holy Spirit, underscoring the intimate and continuous presence of the Spirit.

5.2.2.2 Theological Significance

The indwelling of the Holy Spirit signifies God's permanent presence within believers. This indwelling establishes a personal and ongoing relationship with God, providing the resources needed for spiritual growth and godly living.

5.2.2.3 Practical Implications

- Guidance and Direction: The Spirit guides believers in their daily lives, helping them discern God's will and make wise decisions. John 16:13 promises, "But when He, the Spirit of truth, comes, He will guide you into all the truth."

- Assurance and Comfort: The indwelling Spirit provides assurance of salvation and comfort in times of trouble. Romans 8:16 declares, "The Spirit Himself testifies with our spirit that we are God's children."

- Empowerment for Holy Living: The Spirit's presence empowers believers to live in a manner that honors God. Galatians 5:16 encourages, "So I say, walk by the Spirit, and you will not gratify the desires of the flesh."

5.2.3 Sanctification

Sanctification is the process by which the Holy Spirit makes believers holy, conforming them to the image of Christ. This work involves both initial sanctification at conversion and progressive sanctification throughout the believer's life.

5.2.3.1 Biblical Basis

1 Thessalonians 4:3 states, "It is God's will that you should be sanctified: that you should avoid sexual immorality." This verse underscores that sanctification is God's will for every believer.

Galatians 5:22-23 describes the fruit of the Spirit, which is the evidence of sanctification: "But the fruit of the Spirit is love, joy, peace, forbearance, kindness, goodness, faithfulness, gentleness and self-control."

5.2.3.2 Theological Significance

Sanctification is a vital aspect of the Christian life, reflecting the believer's growth in holiness and conformity to Christ. It is both a divine work of the Spirit and a cooperative effort by the believer to pursue righteousness.

5.2.3.3 Practical Implications

- Transformation of Character: The Holy Spirit works to transform the believer's character, producing the fruit of the Spirit and enabling them to reflect Christ's likeness.

- Victory Over Sin: Through the Spirit's power, believers can overcome sinful habits and live in obedience to God's commands. Romans 8:13 encourages, "For if you live according to the flesh, you will die; but if by the Spirit you put to death the misdeeds of the body, you will live."

- Growth in Grace: Sanctification involves continuous growth in grace and spiritual maturity. Believers are called to cooperate with the Spirit's work by engaging in spiritual disciplines such as prayer, Bible study, and fellowship.

5.2.4 Empowerment

The Holy Spirit empowers believers for service, providing the gifts and strength needed to fulfill God's purposes. This empowerment is essential for effective ministry and witness.

5.2.4.1 Biblical Basis

Acts 1:8 promises, "But you will receive power when the Holy Spirit comes on you, and you will be my witnesses in Jerusalem, and in all Judea and Samaria, and to the ends of the earth." This empowerment enables believers to carry out the Great Commission.

1 Corinthians 12:4-7 explains the distribution of spiritual gifts: "There are different kinds of gifts, but the same Spirit distributes them. There are different kinds of service, but the same Lord. There are different kinds of working, but in all of them and in everyone it is the same God at work. Now to each one the manifestation of the Spirit is given for the common good."

5.2.4.2 Theological Significance

The empowerment of the Holy Spirit equips believers for the diverse tasks and callings within the body of Christ. Spiritual gifts are given for the edification of the church and the advancement of God's kingdom.

5.2.4.3 Practical Implications

- Effective Witness: The Spirit's empowerment enables believers to boldly and effectively share the gospel. Acts 4:31 records, "After they prayed, the place where they were meeting was shaken. And they were all filled with the Holy Spirit and spoke the word of God boldly."

- Service in the Church: Spiritual gifts are given for the benefit of the church. Believers are called to use their gifts to serve one another and build up the body of Christ (1 Peter 4:10).

- Strength for Ministry: The Holy Spirit provides the strength and ability needed for various ministries. Philippians 4:13 affirms, "I can do all this through Him who gives me strength."

5.2.5 Conclusion

The work of the Holy Spirit is comprehensive, encompassing regeneration, indwelling, sanctification, and empowerment. Through regeneration, the Spirit brings new life to believers, making them new creations in Christ. The indwelling of the Spirit assures believers of God's presence and provides guidance and comfort. Sanctification involves the Spirit's ongoing work to transform believers into the likeness of Christ, producing holiness and spiritual maturity. Empowerment equips believers for effective service and witness, distributing spiritual gifts for the edification of the church.

Understanding the work of the Holy Spirit deepens believers' appreciation for His active presence and power in their lives. It encourages a responsive and cooperative relationship with the Spirit, fostering spiritual growth and effective ministry. As we continue to explore systematic theology, the doctrine of the Holy Spirit remains central to our understanding of God's work in and through His people.

5.3 The Gifts of the Spirit

The gifts of the Spirit are special abilities given by the Holy Spirit to believers for the purpose of building up the church and advancing God's kingdom. These gifts vary widely but each is essential for the health and growth of the body of Christ. In this chapter, we will explore the biblical basis for spiritual gifts, the different types of gifts, their purposes, and practical implications for the life of the church.

5.3.1 Biblical Basis for Spiritual Gifts

The New Testament provides a detailed understanding of spiritual gifts, emphasizing their divine origin and purpose.

5.3.1.1 Key Passages

1 Corinthians 12:4-11 offers a foundational description of spiritual gifts: "There are different kinds of gifts, but the same Spirit distributes them. There are different kinds of service, but the same Lord. There are different kinds of working, but in all of them and in everyone it is the same God at work. Now to each one the manifestation of the Spirit is given for the common good. To one there is given through the Spirit a message of wisdom, to another a message of knowledge by means of the same Spirit, to another faith by the same Spirit, to another gift of healing by that one Spirit, to another miraculous power, to another prophecy, to another distinguishing between spirits, to another speaking in different kinds of tongues, and to still another the interpretation of tongues. All these are the work of one and the same Spirit, and He distributes them to each one, just as He determines."

Romans 12:6-8 and Ephesians 4:11-12 also discuss spiritual gifts, providing additional insights into their variety and purposes. Romans 12:6-8 states, "We have different gifts, according to the grace given to each of us. If your gift is prophesying, then prophesy in accordance with your faith; if it is serving, then serve; if it is teaching, then teach; if it is to encourage, then give encouragement; if it is giving, then give generously; if it is to lead, do it diligently; if it is to show mercy, do it cheerfully."

Ephesians 4:11-12 highlights specific leadership gifts: "So Christ Himself gave the apostles, the prophets, the evangelists, the pastors, and teachers, to equip His people for works of service, so that the body of Christ may be built up."

5.3.1.2 The Source of Spiritual Gifts

Spiritual gifts are given by the Holy Spirit according to His will and purpose. 1 Corinthians 12:11 emphasizes, "All these are the work of one and the same Spirit, and He distributes them to each one, just as He determines." This underscores the divine sovereignty in the distribution of gifts and the intentionality behind their allocation.

5.3.2 Types of Spiritual Gifts

The New Testament identifies a variety of spiritual gifts, which can be broadly categorized into three groups: revelatory gifts, speaking gifts, and serving gifts.

5.3.2.1 Revelatory Gifts

Revelatory gifts involve receiving and communicating God's revelation to the church. These include:

- Prophecy: The gift of prophecy involves speaking forth God's message under the inspiration of the Holy Spirit. Prophets provide guidance, correction, and encouragement (1 Corinthians 14:3).

- Word of Wisdom: This gift involves imparting wise counsel and practical insights, often in complex situations (1 Corinthians 12:8).

- Word of Knowledge: The word of knowledge is the ability to understand and communicate specific information that could not be known apart from divine revelation (1 Corinthians 12:8).

- Distinguishing Between Spirits: This gift enables a believer to discern the spiritual origin of messages or activities, whether they are from the Holy Spirit, human spirits, or demonic spirits (1 Corinthians 12:10).

5.3.2.2 Speaking Gifts

Speaking gifts involve the proclamation of God's truth and the building up of the church through teaching and exhortation. These include:

- Teaching: The gift of teaching involves explaining and applying God's Word in a clear and understandable way (Romans 12:7).

- Exhortation: Also known as encouragement, this gift involves motivating and inspiring others to live out their faith (Romans 12:8).

- Tongues and Interpretation of Tongues: Speaking in tongues is the ability to speak in a language unknown to the speaker, often for the purpose of prayer or worship. Interpretation of tongues involves translating the message spoken in tongues for the edification of the church (1 Corinthians 12:10).

5.3.2.3 Serving Gifts

Serving gifts involves practical acts of service and administration within the church. These include:

- Service: The gift of service involves meeting practical needs and assisting in various tasks within the church (Romans 12:7).

- Giving: The gift of giving involves the capacity and willingness to generously support the work of the church and assist those in need (Romans 12:8).

- Leadership: The gift of leadership involves guiding and directing the church in a manner that promotes spiritual growth and organizational effectiveness (Romans 12:8).

- Mercy: The gift of mercy involves showing compassion and care to those who are suffering or in need (Romans 12:8).

- Helps: Similar to the gift of service, the gift of help involves assisting others in their ministry tasks (1 Corinthians 12:28).

- Administration: The gift of administration involves organizing and managing church activities and resources effectively (1 Corinthians 12:28).

5.3.3 Purposes of Spiritual Gifts

Spiritual gifts are given for specific purposes that contribute to the health and mission of the church.

5.3.3.1 Edification of the Church

Spiritual gifts are intended to build up the body of Christ. Ephesians 4:12-13 explains that gifts are given "to equip His people for works of service, so that the body of Christ may be built up until we all reach unity in the faith and in the knowledge of the Son of God and become mature, attaining to the whole measure of the fullness of Christ." The edification of the church involves strengthening believers in their faith, promoting unity, and fostering spiritual maturity.

5.3.3.2 Advancement of God's Kingdom

Spiritual gifts play a crucial role in advancing God's kingdom by enabling effective ministry and witness. Acts 1:8 emphasizes the empowerment for mission: "But you will receive power when the Holy Spirit comes on you; and you will be my witnesses in Jerusalem, and in all Judea and

Samaria, and to the ends of the earth." Through the use of spiritual gifts, believers are equipped to share the gospel, disciple new believers, and engage in various forms of ministry that extend God's reign.

5.3.3.3 Service to Others

Spiritual gifts are also given for the purpose of serving others. 1 Peter 4:10 encourages believers to use their gifts to serve one another: "Each of you should use whatever gift you have received to serve others, as faithful stewards of God's grace in its various forms." This service involves meeting practical needs, providing encouragement, and demonstrating God's love through tangible actions.

5.3.4 Practical Implications for the Church

Understanding and utilizing spiritual gifts has significant practical implications for the life and ministry of the church.

5.3.4.1 Discovery and Development of Gifts

Believers are encouraged to discover and develop their spiritual gifts. This involves seeking God's guidance, engaging in various forms of ministry, and receiving confirmation from the church community. Romans 12:6-8 exhorts believers to use their gifts according to the grace given to them, indicating that each gift should be exercised diligently and faithfully.

5.3.4.2 Use of Gifts in Unity and Diversity

The diversity of spiritual gifts reflects the diversity within the body of Christ. 1 Corinthians 12:12-14 illustrates this diversity: "Just as a body, though one, has many parts, but all its many parts form one body, so it is with Christ. For we were all baptized by one Spirit so as to form one body—whether Jews or Gentiles, slave or free—and we were all given the one Spirit to drink. Even so the body is not made up of one part but of many." The church should celebrate this diversity and encourage the use of gifts in a manner that promotes unity and mutual edification.

5.3.4.3 Avoiding Misuse and Neglect of Gifts

Believers must guard against the misuse and neglect of spiritual gifts. Misuse occurs when gifts are exercised for personal gain or recognition rather than for the common good. Neglect occurs when gifts are not utilized, leading to a lack of growth and vitality in the church. 1 Timothy 4:14 and 2 Timothy 1:6 both encourage believers not to neglect their gifts but to use them for the benefit of the church.

5.3.4.4 Encouraging and Supporting One Another

The church should foster an environment where spiritual gifts are encouraged and supported. This involves providing opportunities for believers to use their gifts, offering training and mentorship, and recognizing the contributions of each member. Hebrews 10:24-25 urges believers to "consider how we may spur one another on toward love and good deeds, not giving up meeting together, as some are in the habit of doing, but encouraging one another—and all the more as you see the Day approaching."

5.3.5 Conclusion

The gifts of the Spirit are essential for the edification of the church and the advancement of God's kingdom. These gifts, bestowed by the Holy Spirit, enable believers to serve one another, build up

the body of Christ, and carry out the mission of the church. Understanding the variety and purpose of spiritual gifts enhances the effectiveness of ministry and promotes unity and maturity within the church.

Believers are called to discover, develop, and use their spiritual gifts faithfully and diligently. By doing so, they contribute to the health and growth of the church and participate in the fulfillment of God's redemptive plan. As we continue to explore systematic theology, the doctrine of the Holy Spirit and His gifts remains central to our understanding of God's work in and through His people.

CHAPTER 06

THE CREATION OF HUMANITY

6.1 The Creation of Humanity

The doctrine of humanity, or anthropology, examines the nature, purpose, and destiny of human beings from a biblical perspective. Central to this doctrine is the belief that humans are created in the image of God (imago Dei), a concept that endows humanity with inherent dignity and worth. This image encompasses rationality, morality, creativity, and the capacity for relationships. In this chapter, we will explore the biblical basis for the creation of humanity, the implications of being made in the image of God, and the practical significance of this doctrine.

6.1.1 Biblical Basis for the Creation of Humanity

The creation of humanity is a fundamental aspect of the biblical narrative, emphasizing God's intentional and purposeful act in bringing humans into existence.

6.1.1.1 Genesis Account

The primary biblical account of human creation is found in Genesis 1:26-27: "Then God said, 'Let us make mankind in our image, in our likeness, so that they may rule over the fish in the sea and the birds in the sky, over the livestock and all the wild animals, and over all the creatures that move along the ground.' So God created mankind in His own image, in the image of God He created them; male and female He created them." This passage highlights several key elements:

- Divine Deliberation: The phrase "Let us make" indicates a deliberate and communal act of creation, reflecting the Trinitarian nature of God.

- Imago Dei: Humans are created in the "image of God," a unique designation that sets them apart from the rest of creation.

- Dominion: Humans are given authority to rule over other creatures, signifying their role as stewards of God's creation.

- Gender: The creation of humans as "male and female" underscores the importance of both genders in reflecting the image of God.

Genesis 2 provides a more detailed account of human creation, emphasizing the personal and intimate nature of God's creative work. Genesis 2:7 states, "Then the Lord God formed a man from the dust of the ground and breathed into his nostrils the breath of life, and the man became a living being." This verse highlights the physical and spiritual dimensions of human life, illustrating the direct involvement of God in creating humanity.

6.1.1.2 Other Biblical References

Other biblical passages affirm and expand upon the creation of humanity in God's image. Psalm 8:4-5 reflects on human dignity and worth: "What is mankind that you are mindful of them, human beings that you care for them? You have made them a little lower than the angels and crowned them with glory and honor." This psalm underscores the elevated status of humans in the created order.

James 3:9 highlights the moral implications of the imago Dei: "With the tongue we praise our Lord and Father, and with it we curse human beings, who have been made in God's likeness." This verse emphasizes the need to respect and honor all people because they are made in God's image.

6.1.2 Implications of Being Made in the Image of God

Being made in the image of God has profound implications for the nature, purpose, and value of human life. This concept encompasses various dimensions of human existence, including rationality, morality, creativity, and relationality.

6.1.2.1 Rationality

Humans possess rationality, the ability to think, reason, and make decisions. This intellectual capacity reflects God's own wisdom and knowledge. Isaiah 1:18 invites, "Come now, let us reason together, says the Lord." The capacity for rational thought enables humans to engage in scientific inquiry, philosophical reflection, and theological study, all of which contribute to a deeper understanding of God and His creation.

6.1.2.2 Morality

Humans are endowed with a moral sense, the ability to discern right from wrong. This moral awareness reflects God's own holiness and justice. Romans 2:14-15 explains, "Indeed, when Gentiles, who do not have the law, do by nature things required by the law, they are a law for themselves, even though they do not have the law. They show that the requirements of the law are written on their hearts, their consciences also bearing witness, and their thoughts sometimes accusing them and at other times even defending them." This innate sense of morality calls humans to live in accordance with God's standards and to pursue justice, compassion, and integrity.

6.1.2.3 Creativity

Humans possess creativity, the ability to imagine, design, and create. This creative capacity reflects God's own creativity, as seen in the beauty and diversity of the natural world. Exodus 35:31-32 describes Bezalel, an artisan filled with the Spirit of God: "And He has filled him with the Spirit of God, with wisdom, with understanding, with knowledge and with all kinds of skills—to make artistic designs for work in gold, silver, and bronze." Human creativity is expressed in art, music, literature, technology, and other forms of cultural production, enriching human life and reflecting God's creative glory.

6.1.2.4 Relationality

Humans are inherently relational beings, created for relationships with God and with one another. This relational capacity reflects the communal nature of the Trinity. Genesis 2:18 states, "The Lord God said, 'It is not good for the man to be alone. I will make a helper suitable for him.'" Relationships are essential for human flourishing, encompassing family, friendships, and community life. The greatest commandments, to love God and to love one's neighbor (Matthew 22:37-40), highlight the centrality of relationships in fulfilling God's purpose for humanity.

6.1.3 Practical Significance of the Imago Dei

The doctrine of the imago Dei has significant practical implications for how humans view themselves, others, and their responsibilities in the world.

6.1.3.1 Human Dignity and Worth

Every human being possesses inherent dignity and worth because they are made in the image of God. This truth forms the basis for the biblical understanding of human rights and the sanctity of life. Genesis 9:6 underscores the seriousness of taking human life: "Whoever sheds human blood, by humans shall their blood be shed; for in the image of God has God made mankind." Respecting and valuing every person, regardless of race, gender, age, or social status, is a fundamental Christian duty.

6.1.3.2 Ethical Behavior

The imago Dei calls humans to live ethically, reflecting God's character in their actions. This involves pursuing justice, practicing mercy, and walking humbly with God (Micah 6:8). Ethical behavior extends to all areas of life, including personal conduct, social relationships, and professional responsibilities. Christians are called to be salt and light in the world (Matthew 5:13-16), exemplifying God's righteousness and love in their interactions with others.

6.1.3.3 Stewardship of Creation

Being made in the image of God includes the responsibility to steward and care for creation. Genesis 1:28 gives humans the mandate to "fill the earth and subdue it. Rule over the fish in the sea and the birds in the sky and over every living creature that moves on the ground." This stewardship involves managing the earth's resources wisely, protecting the environment, and promoting the well-being of all creation. Christians are called to reflect God's care for the world by engaging in sustainable practices and advocating for environmental justice.

6.1.3.4 Pursuit of Relationships

The relational nature of the imago Dei emphasizes the importance of building and nurturing relationships. Christians are called to love God with all their heart, soul, and mind, and to love their neighbors as themselves (Matthew 22:37-39). This involves fostering a genuine community, seeking reconciliation, and demonstrating hospitality and compassion. Healthy relationships within families, churches, and society are vital for reflecting God's relational nature and fulfilling His purposes.

6.1.4 The Distortion and Restoration of the Imago Dei

While the imago Dei endows humans with dignity and purpose, it has been marred by sin. However, through Christ, the image of God is being restored in believers.

6.1.4.1 The Impact of Sin

The fall of humanity into sin has distorted the image of God. Genesis 3 recounts the disobedience of Adam and Eve, resulting in broken relationships with God, each other, and creation. Romans 3:23 states, "for all have sinned and fall short of the glory of God." This fallen state affects every aspect of human existence, including rationality, morality, creativity, and relationality.

6.1.4.2 Restoration through Christ

Jesus Christ, the perfect image of God (Colossians 1:15), came to restore the imago Dei in humanity. Through His life, death, and resurrection, believers are redeemed and transformed into His likeness. 2 Corinthians 3:18 explains, "And we all, who with unveiled faces contemplate the Lord's glory, are being transformed into His image with ever-increasing glory, which comes from the Lord, who is the Spirit." The process of sanctification involves the Holy Spirit working with believers to renew and restore the image of God.

6.1.4.3 The Future Fulfillment

The restoration of the imago Dei will be fully realized in the new creation. 1 John 3:2 promises, "Dear friends, now we are children of God, and what we will be has not yet been made known. But we know that when Christ appears, we shall be like Him, for we shall see Him as He is." The ultimate destiny of humanity is to be fully conformed to the image of Christ, enjoying perfect fellowship with God and each other.

6.1.5 Conclusion

The creation of humanity in the image of God is a foundational doctrine that shapes the Christian understanding of human nature, purpose, and destiny. Being made in the imago Dei endows humans with inherent dignity and worth, calls them to live ethically and relationally, and entrusts them with the stewardship of creation. Despite the distortion of the image by sin, the redemptive work of Christ provides the means for its restoration. As believers grow in their likeness to Christ, they reflect the glory of God and fulfill their purpose as His image-bearers. The doctrine of the imago Dei remains central to understanding humanity's place in God's plan and their relationship with Him and His creation.

6.2 The Fall of Humanity

The fall of humanity is a pivotal event in the biblical narrative, describing humanity's rebellion against God through the disobedience of Adam and Eve. This act of defiance, recorded in Genesis 3, introduced sin and its consequences into the world, fundamentally altering human existence and the created order. In this chapter, we will explore the biblical account of the fall, its theological significance, and its profound impact on humanity and creation.

6.2.1 The Biblical Account of the Fall

The fall of humanity is detailed in Genesis 3, where the first humans, Adam and Eve, succumb to temptation and disobey God's command.

6.2.1.1 The Setting

Genesis 3 begins by introducing the serpent, a cunning creature that serves as the tempter. The serpent engages Eve in conversation, questioning God's command and insinuating doubt about God's intentions. Genesis 3:1 states, "Now the serpent was more crafty than any of the wild animals the Lord God had made. He said to the woman, 'Did God really say, 'You must not eat from any tree in the garden'?'"

6.2.1.2 The Temptation and Disobedience

The serpent's strategy involves distorting God's word and appealing to Eve's desires. Genesis 3:4-6 records the critical exchange: "'You will not certainly die,' the serpent said to the woman. 'For God knows that when you eat from it your eyes will be opened, and you will be like God, knowing good and evil.' When the woman saw that the fruit of the tree was good for food and pleasing to the eye, and also desirable for gaining wisdom, she took some and ate it. She also gave some to her husband, who was with her, and he ate it."

This act of eating the forbidden fruit signifies a deliberate choice to disobey God, driven by the desire for autonomy and the pursuit of knowledge apart from God.

6.2.1.3 The Immediate Consequences

The immediate consequences of Adam and Eve's disobedience are described in Genesis 3:7-13. Their eyes are opened, and they become aware of their nakedness, leading to shame and attempts to cover themselves with fig leaves. When God confronts them, they attempt to shift the blame: Adam blames Eve, and Eve blames the serpent.

6.2.1.4 The Divine Judgment

God pronounces judgment on the serpent, Eve, and Adam, detailing the far-reaching consequences of their sin. Genesis 3:14-19 outlines these judgments:

- Serpent: The serpent is cursed above all animals and destined to crawl on its belly. Enmity is established between the serpent and humanity, culminating in the promise of a future redeemer who will crush the serpent's head (Genesis 3:15).

- Eve: Eve's judgment involves increased pain in childbirth and a distorted relationship with her husband, marked by conflict and desire (Genesis 3:16).

- Adam: Adam's judgment affects his relationship with the ground, introducing toil and hardship in working the land. Death is introduced as the ultimate consequence of sin: "for dust you are and to dust you will return" (Genesis 3:17-19).

6.2.1.5 Expulsion from Eden

Adam and Eve are expelled from the Garden of Eden, signifying their separation from God's immediate presence and the loss of their original home. Genesis 3:23-24 describes this expulsion and the placement of cherubim to guard the way to the tree of life, preventing their return.

6.2.2 Theological Significance of the Fall

The fall of humanity is a foundational event with profound theological implications. It explains the origin of sin, the nature of human depravity, and the necessity of redemption.

6.2.2.1 The Origin of Sin

The fall introduces sin into the world, defined as rebellion against God's will and order. Romans 5:12 explains, "Therefore, just as sin entered the world through one man, and death through sin, and in this way death came to all people because all sinned." Sin is not merely a violation of

God's commandments but a fundamental breach in the relationship between God and humanity.

6.2.2.2 Human Depravity

The fall results in the total depravity of humanity, meaning that every aspect of human nature is tainted by sin. This condition affects the mind, will, emotions, and body. Jeremiah 17:9 states, "The heart is deceitful above all things and beyond cure. Who can understand it?" Human beings are inclined toward sin, unable to achieve righteousness on their own.

6.2.2.3 The Necessity of Redemption

The fall underscores the necessity of redemption. Humanity's broken relationship with God requires divine intervention to restore fellowship. Romans 3:23-24 declares, "for all have sinned and fall short of the glory of God, and all are justified freely by His grace through the redemption that came by Christ Jesus." The promise of a redeemer in Genesis 3:15 points to Jesus Christ, who fulfills this promise through His life, death, and resurrection.

6.2.3 The Impact of the Fall

The fall has far-reaching consequences that affect all aspects of human existence and the created order.

6.2.3.1 Spiritual Death

The primary consequence of the fall is spiritual death, defined as separation from God. Ephesians 2:1-2 describes humanity's condition: "As for you, you were dead in your transgressions and sins, in which you used to live when you followed the ways of this world and of the ruler of the kingdom of the air, the spirit who is now at work in those who are disobedient." Spiritual death results in a loss of fellowship with God and the need for spiritual regeneration.

6.2.3.2 Physical Death and Suffering

The fall introduces physical death and suffering into the world. Romans 6:23 states, "For the wages of sin is death, but the gift of God is eternal life in Christ Jesus our Lord." The inevitability of death and the presence of suffering and disease are direct results of sin's entry into the world.

6.2.3.3 Moral Corruption

Humanity's moral nature is corrupted by sin, leading to widespread wickedness and injustice. Romans 1:28-32 depicts the moral decay resulting from rejecting God: "They have become filled with every kind of wickedness, evil, greed and depravity. They are full of envy, murder, strife, deceit and malice. They are gossips, slanderers, God-haters, insolent, arrogant and boastful; they invent ways of doing evil; they disobey their parents; they have no understanding, no fidelity, no love, no mercy."

6.2.3.4 Relational Strife

The fall distorts human relationships, introducing conflict and strife. The judgment on Eve includes increased pain in relationships, particularly within the family (Genesis 3:16). This relational brokenness extends to all human interactions, contributing to societal discord and interpersonal conflict.

6.2.3.5 Environmental Decay

The fall affects the entire created order, resulting in environmental decay and disorder. Romans 8:20-22 describes creation's suffering: "For the creation was subjected to frustration, not by its own choice, but by the will of the one who subjected it, in hope that the creation itself will be liberated from its bondage to decay and brought into the freedom and glory of the children of God. We know that the whole creation has been groaning as in the pains of childbirth right up to the present time." The natural world experiences the consequences of human sin, including natural disasters and ecological degradation.

6.2.4 Hope and Redemption

Despite the devastating impact of the fall, the biblical narrative offers hope through God's redemptive plan. This hope is anchored in the promise of a redeemer and the ultimate restoration of all things.

6.2.4.1 The Protoevangelium

Genesis 3:15, often referred to as the protoevangelium or "first gospel," contains the first promise of redemption. God declares to the serpent, "And I will put enmity between you and the woman, and between your offspring and hers; he will crush your head, and you will strike his heel." This promise foreshadows the victory of Jesus Christ over sin and Satan, providing the foundation for the entire redemptive narrative.

6.2.4.2 The Work of Christ

The life, death, and resurrection of Jesus Christ fulfill the promise of redemption. Through His sacrificial death, Jesus atones for sin, reconciling humanity to God. Romans 5:18-19 explains, "Consequently, just as one trespass resulted in condemnation for all people, so also one righteous act resulted in justification and life for all people. For just as through the disobedience of the one man the many were made sinners, so also through the obedience of the one man, the many will be made righteous."

6.2.4.3 The Restoration of Creation

The ultimate hope for humanity and creation is the restoration of all things in Christ. Revelation 21:1-4 depicts this future restoration: "Then I saw 'a new heaven and a new earth,' for the first heaven and the first earth had passed away, and there was no longer any sea. I saw the Holy City, the new Jerusalem, coming down out of heaven from God, prepared as a bride beautifully dressed for her husband. And I heard a loud voice from the throne saying, 'Look! God's dwelling place is now among the people, and He will dwell with them. They will be His people, and God Himself will be with them and be their God. He will wipe every tear from their eyes. There will be no more death or mourning or crying or pain, for the old order of things has passed away."

6.2.5 Practical Implications

Understanding the fall of humanity has significant practical implications for Christian living and ministry.

6.2.5.1 Acknowledgment of Human Sinfulness

Recognizing the reality of the fall requires an acknowledgment of human sinfulness and the need for repentance. Romans 3:23 reminds us, "For all have sinned and fall short of the glory of God." This acknowledgment is the first step toward receiving God's grace and forgiveness.

6.2.5.2 Dependence on God's Grace

The fall underscores the necessity of God's grace for salvation and transformation. Ephesians 2:8-9 emphasizes, "For it is by grace you have been saved, through faith—and this is not from yourselves, it is the gift of God—not by works so that no one can boast." Believers are called to live in humble dependence on God's grace, recognizing that their righteousness comes from Him.

6.2.5.3 Commitment to Holiness and Righteousness

In response to God's grace, believers are called to pursue holiness and righteousness. 1 Peter 1:15-16 exhorts, "But just as He who called you is holy, so be holy in all you do; for it is written: 'Be holy because I am holy.'" This commitment involves rejecting sinful behaviors and cultivating a life that reflects God's character.

6.2.5.4 Engagement in Redemptive Mission

Understanding the fall motivates believers to engage in God's redemptive mission. This includes sharing the gospel, serving others, and working toward justice and reconciliation. 2 Corinthians 5:18-20 calls believers to be ambassadors of reconciliation: "All this is from God, who reconciled us to Himself through Christ and gave us the ministry of reconciliation: that God was reconciling the world to Himself in Christ, not counting people's sins against them. And He has committed to us the message of reconciliation. We are therefore Christ's ambassadors, as though God were making His appeal through us."

6.2.6 Conclusion

The fall of humanity is a central event in the biblical narrative, explaining the origin of sin and its pervasive impact on human existence and the created order. Through the disobedience of Adam and Eve, sin entered the world, resulting in spiritual and physical death, moral corruption, relational strife, and environmental decay. Despite these devastating consequences, the Bible offers hope through God's redemptive plan, culminating in the work of Jesus Christ and the ultimate restoration of all things.

Understanding the fall underscores the need for repentance, dependence on God's grace, and commitment to holiness. It also motivates believers to participate in God's redemptive mission, proclaiming the gospel and working toward the reconciliation of all creation. As we continue to explore systematic theology, the doctrine of the fall remains foundational to our understanding of humanity's condition and God's gracious provision for salvation and restoration.

6.3 The Nature of Sin

Sin is a fundamental concept in Christian theology, referring to any thought, word, or deed that falls short of God's standard of holiness. Understanding the nature of sin is crucial for comprehending humanity's separation from God, the need for redemption, and the moral and spiritual implications of human actions. In this chapter, we will explore the biblical definition of sin, its theological significance, its consequences, and its pervasive effects on human existence.

6.3.1 Biblical Definition of Sin

The Bible provides a comprehensive understanding of sin, encompassing various aspects of human behavior and conditions that deviate from God's will and character.

6.3.1.1 Sin as Transgression

Sin is often described as transgression, which means to cross a boundary or violate a command. 1 John 3:4 states, "Everyone who sins breaks the law; in fact, sin is lawlessness." This emphasizes that sin involves breaking God's commandments and acting contrary to His revealed will.

6.3.1.2 Sin as Missing the Mark

The Greek word for sin, "hamartia," literally means "missing the mark." This term conveys the idea of failing to meet God's perfect standard of righteousness. Romans 3:23 declares, "for all have sinned and fall short of the glory of God." Sin is not merely a matter of external actions but also includes internal attitudes and motivations that fall short of God's holiness.

6.3.1.3 Sin as Rebellion

Sin is also depicted as a rebellion against God. Isaiah 1:2 portrays Israel's sin in this light: "Hear me, you heavens! Listen, earth! For the Lord has spoken: 'I reared children and brought them up, but they have rebelled against me.'"

Rebellion signifies a deliberate and defiant opposition to God's authority and rule.

6.3.1.4 Sin as Iniquity

The term "iniquity" refers to moral crookedness or perversity. Psalm 51:2-3 uses this term in David's confession: "Wash away all my iniquity and cleanse me from my sin. For I know my transgressions and my sin is always before me." Iniquity highlights the corrupt and twisted nature of sin that distorts human character and actions.

6.3.2 Theological Significance of Sin

Understanding the nature of sin is essential for grasping the broader theological framework of the Bible, including the need for salvation and the work of Christ.

6.3.2.1 The Universality of Sin

The Bible teaches that all humans are sinners by nature and by choice. Romans 3:23 affirms, "for all have sinned and fall short of the glory of God." This universality of sin underscores the pervasive and inherent nature of sin in human beings, affecting every individual without exception.

6.3.2.2 The Origin of Sin

Sin entered the world through the disobedience of Adam and Eve, as described in Genesis 3. Romans 5:12 explains, "Therefore, just as sin entered the world through one man, and death through sin, and in this way death came to all people because all sinned." This original sin brought corruption and death into the world, affecting all of Adam's descendants.

6.3.2.3 The Depravity of Sin

Sin is not merely a series of isolated actions but a condition of the heart. Jeremiah 17:9 declares, "The heart is deceitful above all things and beyond cure. Who can understand it?" Human depravity means that sin affects every aspect of human nature, including thoughts, emotions, desires, and will. This total depravity does not mean that humans are as sinful as they could be, but that sin has touched every part of their being.

6.3.2.4 The Offensiveness of Sin

Sin is fundamentally offensive to God's holy nature. Habakkuk 1:13 states, "Your eyes are too pure to look on evil; you cannot tolerate wrongdoing." Sin is an affront to God's holiness, justice, and righteousness, necessitating divine judgment and separation from God.

6.3.3 Consequences of Sin

The consequences of sin are severe and multifaceted, affecting individuals, relationships, and the entire created order.

6.3.3.1 Spiritual Death

The primary consequence of sin is spiritual death, which is separation from God. Ephesians 2:1 describes the state of those living in sin: "As for you, you were dead in your transgressions and sins." Spiritual death signifies a loss of fellowship with God and the inability to respond to Him apart from divine intervention.

6.3.3.2 Physical Death

Sin also brings about physical death. Romans 6:23 declares, "For the wages of sin is death, but the gift of God is eternal life in Christ Jesus our Lord." Physical death is a direct result of sin and serves as a reminder of the brokenness and mortality of human life.

6.3.3.3 Relational Estrangement

Sin causes estrangement in human relationships, leading to conflict, betrayal, and injustice. James 4:1-2 explains, "What causes fights and quarrels among you? Don't they come from your desires that battle within you? You desire but do not have, so you kill. You covet but you cannot get what you want, so you quarrel and fight." Sin disrupts harmony and fosters division in families, communities, and nations.

6.3.3.4 Environmental Degradation

The consequences of sin extend to the natural world. Genesis 3:17-18 describes the curse on the ground due to

Adam's sin: "Cursed is the ground because of you; through painful toil, you will eat food from it all the days of your life. It will produce thorns and thistles for you, and you will eat the plants of the field." Romans 8:20-22 speaks of creation's subjection to frustration and its groaning for redemption.

6.3.4 The Pervasive Effects of Sin

Sin's effects permeate every aspect of human existence and the world, creating a need for redemption and restoration.

6.3.4.1 Personal Pervasiveness

Sin affects the individual on a deeply personal level, corrupting thoughts, emotions, and actions. Paul laments this pervasive influence in Romans 7:18-19: "For I know that good itself does not dwell in me, that is, in my sinful nature. For I have the desire to do what is good, but I cannot carry it out. For I do not do the good I want to do, but the evil I do not want to do—this I keep on doing."

6.3.4.2 Societal Pervasiveness

Sin affects society at large, manifesting in systemic injustices, exploitation, and violence. Micah 6:12 denounces social corruption: "Your rich people are violent; your inhabitants are liars and their tongues speak deceitfully." Sinful structures and practices perpetuate suffering and oppression.

6.3.4.3 Cosmic Pervasiveness

Sin's impact extends to the cosmos, affecting the entire created order. Romans 8:22 states, "We know that the whole creation has been groaning as in the pains of childbirth right up to the present time." This cosmic dimension of sin underscores the comprehensive scope of its effects and the need for universal restoration.

6.3.5 Hope and Redemption

Despite the pervasive and devastating nature of sin, the biblical narrative offers hope through God's redemptive plan, centered on Jesus Christ.

6.3.5.1 The Promise of Redemption

From the moment of the fall, God promised redemption. Genesis 3:15 contains the protoevangelium, the first gospel promise, indicating a future redeemer who will crush the serpent's head. This promise is fulfilled in Jesus Christ, who came to save humanity from sin.

6.3.5.2 The Work of Christ

Jesus Christ's life, death, and resurrection provide the remedy for sin. 2 Corinthians 5:21 explains, "God made Him who had no sin to be sin for us, so that in Him we might become the righteousness of God." Christ's atoning sacrifice satisfies God's justice, reconciles sinners to God, and breaks the power of sin.

6.3.5.3 The Role of the Holy Spirit

The Holy Spirit plays a vital role in applying the work of Christ to believers. Through the Spirit's regenerating and sanctifying work, believers are transformed and empowered to live in righteousness. Romans 8:1-2 declares, "Therefore, there is now no condemnation for those who are in Christ Jesus because through Christ Jesus the law of the Spirit who gives life has set you free from the law of sin and death."

6.3.5.4 The Hope of Restoration

The ultimate hope for humanity and creation is the restoration of all things in Christ. Revelation 21:4-5 describes this future restoration: "He will wipe every tear from their eyes. There will be no more death or mourning or crying or pain, for the old order of things has passed away. He who was seated on the throne said, 'I am making everything new!'" This eschatological hope assures believers of the final defeat of sin and the renewal of creation.

6.3.6 Practical Implications

Understanding the nature of sin has significant practical implications for Christian living and ministry.

6.3.6.1 Confession and Repentance

Believers are called to confess their sins and repent. 1 John 1:9 promises, "If we confess our sins, He is faithful and just and will forgive us our sins and purify us from all unrighteousness." Confession and repentance are essential for maintaining a right relationship with God.

6.3.6.2 Pursuit of Holiness

In response to God's grace, believers are called to pursue holiness and resist sin. 1 Peter 1:15-16 exhorts, "But just as He who called you is holy, so be holy in all you do; for it is written: 'Be holy because I am holy.'" This pursuit involves reliance on the Holy Spirit and engagement in spiritual disciplines.

6.3.6.3 Commitment to Justice and Reconciliation

Understanding sin's societal and relational effects motivates believers to work for justice and reconciliation. Micah 6:8 calls believers to "act justly and to love mercy and to walk humbly with your God." This commitment involves addressing systemic injustices and promoting peace and reconciliation in communities.

6.3.6.4 Hope and Witness

The hope of redemption and restoration empowers believers to bear witness to the gospel. 2 Corinthians 5:20 describes believers as ambassadors for Christ: "We are therefore Christ's ambassadors, as though God were making His appeal through us. We implore you on Christ's behalf: Be reconciled to God." Sharing the message of salvation and living out its implications is central to the Christian witness.

6.3.7 Conclusion

The nature of sin is a crucial aspect of Christian theology, explaining humanity's separation from God and the pervasive effects of sin on individuals, society, and creation. Sin is any thought, word, or deed that falls short of God's standard of holiness, resulting in spiritual and physical death. Despite its devastating impact, the Bible offers hope through the redemptive work of Jesus Christ and the transforming power of the Holy Spirit. Understanding the nature of sin calls believers to confession, repentance, holiness, justice, and witness, as they live in the hope of ultimate restoration in Christ. As we continue to explore systematic theology, the doctrine of sin remains central to understanding the human condition and God's gracious provision for salvation and renewal.

6.4 Redemption and Restoration

The fall of humanity brought sin and its devastating consequences into the world, but God, in His grace and mercy, provided a way of redemption through Jesus Christ. Redemption involves the deliverance from sin and its consequences, and restoration refers to the process of being made new and reconciled to God. This chapter explores the biblical basis, theological significance, and practical implications of redemption and restoration, emphasizing the transformative power of Christ's work.

6.4.1 The Biblical Basis of Redemption

Redemption is a central theme in the Bible, encompassing both the Old and New Testaments. It involves the payment of a ransom to secure the release of someone from bondage or slavery, symbolizing the deliverance from sin through Jesus Christ.

6.4.1.1 Old Testament Foreshadowing

The concept of redemption is foreshadowed in the Old Testament through various types and shadows, most notably the Exodus. In Exodus 6:6, God declares, "Therefore, say to the Israelites: 'I am the Lord, and I will bring you out from under the yoke of the Egyptians. I will free you from being slaves to them, and I will redeem you with an outstretched arm and with mighty acts of judgment.'" The deliverance of Israel from Egypt serves as a prototype of the ultimate redemption through Christ.

The sacrificial system in Leviticus also prefigures the atoning work of Christ. The Day of Atonement (Yom Kippur), described in Leviticus 16, involves the high priest making a sin offering for the people, symbolizing the future atonement accomplished by Jesus.

6.4.1.2 New Testament Fulfillment

The New Testament presents Jesus Christ as the fulfillment of the Old Testament foreshadowing, the ultimate Redeemer who delivers humanity from sin. Ephesians 1:7 states, "In Him we have redemption through His blood, the forgiveness of sins, in accordance with the riches of God's grace."

Romans 3:24-25 further explains, "and all are justified freely by His grace through the redemption that came by Christ Jesus. God presented Christ as a sacrifice of atonement, through the shedding of His blood—to be received by faith." The death and resurrection of Jesus Christ constitute the basis for redemption, providing forgiveness and reconciliation with God.

6.4.2 The Theological Significance of Redemption

Redemption is not just a transaction but a profound theological reality that encompasses various aspects of salvation, including justification, reconciliation, adoption, and sanctification.

6.4.2.1 Justification

Justification is the act of God declaring sinners righteous based on the atoning work of Christ. Romans 5:1 states, "Therefore, since we have been justified through faith, we have peace with God through our Lord Jesus Christ." Justification involves both the forgiveness of sins and the imputation of Christ's righteousness to believers, restoring their legal standing before God.

6.4.2.2 Reconciliation

Reconciliation refers to the restoration of a broken relationship between God and humanity. 2 Corinthians 5:18-19 explains, "All this is from God, who reconciled us to Himself through Christ and gave us the ministry of reconciliation: that God was reconciling the world to Himself in Christ, not counting people's sins against them." Through Christ, the enmity caused by sin is removed, and believers are brought back into fellowship with God.

6.4.2.3 Adoption

Adoption is the gracious act of God by which believers are made His children. Galatians 4:4-5 states, "But when the set time had fully come, God sent His Son, born of a woman, born under the law, to redeem those under the law, that we might receive adoption to sonship." As adopted children, believers enjoy the privileges of being part of God's family, including intimacy with the Father and the inheritance of eternal life.

6.4.2.4 Sanctification

Sanctification is the process by which believers are made holy, conforming to the image of Christ. It involves both an initial sanctification at conversion and a progressive sanctification throughout the believer's life. 1 Thessalonians 5:23 prays, "May God Himself, the God of peace, sanctify you through and through. May your whole spirit, soul and body be kept blameless at the coming of our Lord Jesus Christ." Sanctification is the work of the Holy Spirit, enabling believers to live in righteousness and holiness.

6.4.3 The Process of Restoration

Restoration is the ongoing work of God in the life of believers, transforming them into new creations and preparing them for eternal life with Him. This process involves spiritual renewal, growth in Christlikeness, and the ultimate restoration of all things.

6.4.3.1 Spiritual Renewal

Spiritual renewal begins with regeneration, the new birth brought about by the Holy Spirit. Titus 3:5 states, "He saved us through the washing of rebirth and renewal by the Holy Spirit." Regeneration marks the beginning of a believer's new life in Christ, characterized by a transformed heart and mind.

2 Corinthians 5:17 emphasizes the transformative nature of this renewal: "Therefore, if anyone is in Christ, the new creation has come: The old has gone, the new is here!" This new creation involves a fundamental change in identity,

desires, and direction, aligning believers with God's will and purposes.

6.4.3.2 Growth in Christlikeness

The restoration process continues as believers grow in Christlikeness, becoming more like Jesus in character and conduct. Romans 8:29 explains, "For those God foreknew He also predestined to be conformed to the image of His Son, that He might be the firstborn among many brothers and sisters." This growth involves the cultivation of the fruit of the Spirit (Galatians 5:22-23) and the practice of spiritual disciplines such as prayer, Bible study, and fellowship.

Ephesians 4:22-24 exhorts believers, "You were taught, with regard to your former way of life, to put off your old self, which is being corrupted by its deceitful desires; to be made new in the attitude of your minds; and to put on the new self, created to be like God in true righteousness and holiness." This process requires intentional effort and cooperation with the Holy Spirit, leading to progressive sanctification and maturity in faith.

6.4.3.3 Ultimate Restoration

The ultimate restoration of all things is a future reality promised in Scripture. Revelation 21:1-4 depicts the new heaven and new earth, where God will dwell with His people: "Then I saw 'a new heaven and a new earth,' for the first heaven and the first earth had passed away, and there was no longer any sea. I saw the Holy City, the new Jerusalem, coming down out of heaven from God, prepared as a bride beautifully dressed for her husband. And I heard a loud voice from the throne saying, 'Look! God's dwelling place is now among the people, and He will dwell with them. They will be His people, and God Himself will be with them and be their God. He will wipe every tear from their eyes. There will be no more death' or mourning or crying or pain, for the old order of things has passed away."

This ultimate restoration involves the renewal of creation, the eradication of sin and its effects, and the fulfillment of God's redemptive plan. Believers will experience perfect fellowship with God and each other, enjoying eternal life in His presence.

6.4.4 Practical Implications of Redemption and Restoration

The truths of redemption and restoration have significant practical implications for the lives of believers, shaping their identity, purpose, and mission.

6.4.4.1 Identity in Christ

Believers' identity is fundamentally transformed by redemption and restoration. They are no longer defined by their past sins or failures but by their new status as children of God and co-heirs with Christ. Galatians 2:20 proclaims, "I have been crucified with Christ and I no longer live, but Christ lives in me. The life I now live in the body, I live by faith in the Son of God, who loved me and gave Himself for me." This new identity empowers believers to live with confidence, purpose, and hope.

6.4.4.2 Purpose and Mission

Redemption and restoration give believers a renewed sense of purpose and mission. They are called to participate in God's redemptive work by sharing the gospel, serving others, and promoting justice and reconciliation. 2 Corinthians 5:20 states, "We are therefore Christ's ambassadors, as though God were making His appeal through us. We implore you on Christ's behalf: Be reconciled to God." Believers are called to be agents of transformation in their communities, reflecting the love and grace of Christ.

6.4.4.3 Holistic Transformation

The process of restoration involves holistic transformation, affecting every aspect of a believer's life. Romans 12:1-2 exhorts, "Therefore, I urge you, brothers and sisters, in view of God's mercy, to offer your bodies as a living sacrifice, holy and pleasing to God—this is your true and proper worship. Do not conform to the pattern of this world, but be transformed by the renewing of your mind. Then you will be able to test and approve what God's will is—His good, pleasing, and perfect will." This transformation includes spiritual, moral, relational, and vocational aspects, leading to a life that honors God in all areas.

6.4.4.4 Hope and Perseverance

The hope of ultimate restoration provides believers with strength and

perseverance in the face of trials and suffering. Romans 8:18 encourages, "I consider that our present sufferings are not worth comparing with the glory that will be revealed in us." This eschatological hope sustains believers, reminding them that their present struggles are temporary and that God's promise of renewal is sure.

6.4.5 Conclusion

Redemption and restoration are central themes in the Christian faith, highlighting God's gracious provision for humanity's deliverance from sin and the ongoing work of renewal in believers' lives. Through the redemptive work of Jesus Christ, believers are justified, reconciled, adopted, and sanctified, becoming new creations in Christ. The process of restoration involves spiritual renewal, growth in Christlikeness, and the ultimate restoration of all things.

Understanding these truths shapes believers' identity, purpose, and mission, empowering them to live transformed lives and participate in God's redemptive work. As we continue to explore systematic theology, the doctrines of redemption and restoration remain foundational to our understanding of God's grace and His plan for humanity and creation.

CHAPTER 07

THE PLAN OF SALVATION

7.1 The Plan of Salvation

The doctrine of salvation, or soteriology, is a central tenet of Christian theology, exploring how God saves individuals from sin and its consequences, granting them eternal life. The plan of salvation is a comprehensive framework that encompasses God's eternal purpose and His redemptive work throughout history. It involves the calling, justification, sanctification, and glorification of believers. In this chapter, we will examine the biblical basis, theological significance, and practical implications of God's plan of salvation.

7.1.1 The Eternal Plan of Salvation

God's plan of salvation was established before the foundation of the world. This divine forethought reflects

God's sovereignty and His gracious intention to redeem humanity.

7.1.1.1 Divine Foreknowledge and Predestination

Ephesians 1:4-5 declares, "For He chose us in Him before the creation of the world to be holy and blameless in His sight. In love He predestined us for adoption to sonship through Jesus Christ, in accordance with His pleasure and will." This passage highlights that God's plan for salvation was conceived in eternity past, rooted in His love and sovereign will.

Romans 8:29-30 further explains, "For those God foreknew He also predestined to be conformed to the image of His Son, that He might be the firstborn among many brothers and sisters. And those He predestined, He also called; those He called, He also justified; those He justified, He also glorified." These verses outline the stages of salvation, emphasizing God's initiative and the assurance of its fulfillment.

7.1.1.2 The Role of Jesus Christ

Central to God's plan of salvation is the person and work of Jesus Christ. 1 Peter 1:20-21 states, "He was chosen before the creation of the world, but was revealed in these last times for your sake. Through Him, you believe in God, who raised Him from the dead and glorified Him, and so your faith and hope are in God." Jesus' sacrificial death and resurrection are the cornerstone of salvation, revealing God's redemptive plan in history.

7.1.2 Calling

Calling is the initial stage in the process of salvation, where God invites individuals to enter into a relationship with Him. This calling can be understood in two ways: general and effectual.

7.1.2.1 General Calling

The general calling refers to the proclamation of the gospel to all people. Matthew 22:14 mentions, "For many are invited, but few are chosen." This invitation is extended to everyone, emphasizing God's desire for all to come to repentance.

7.1.2.2 Effectual Calling

The effectual calling is the work of the Holy Spirit, effectively drawing individuals to faith in Christ. John 6:44 explains, "No one can come to me unless the Father who sent me draws them, and I will raise them up at the last day." This calling results in a positive response, leading to conversion and salvation.

Romans 8:30 reinforces this concept: "And those He predestined, He also called; those He called, He also justified; those He justified, He also glorified." The effectual calling is a decisive act of God that guarantees the believer's subsequent justification and glorification.

7.1.3 Justification

Justification is the legal act by which God declares a sinner righteous on the basis of faith in Jesus Christ. It involves both the forgiveness of sins and the imputation of Christ's righteousness.

7.1.3.1 By Faith Alone

Justification is received through faith alone, apart from works. Romans 3:28 asserts, "For we maintain that a person is justified by faith apart from the works of the law." Faith is the means by which individuals appropriate the benefits of Christ's atoning sacrifice.

7.1.3.2 Imputed Righteousness

Justification involves the imputation of Christ's righteousness to the believer. 2 Corinthians 5:21 explains, "God made Him who had no sin to be sin for us, so that in Him we might become the righteousness of God." This imputation means that Christ's perfect righteousness is credited to the believer, allowing them to stand justified before God.

7.1.3.3 Peace with God

The result of justification is peace with God. Romans 5:1 declares, "Therefore, since we have been justified through faith, we have peace with God through our Lord Jesus Christ." This peace signifies reconciliation with God and the assurance of His favor.

7.1.4 Sanctification

Sanctification is the process by which believers are made holy, being conformed to the image of Christ. It involves both positional sanctification, which occurs at conversion, and progressive sanctification, which continues throughout the believer's life.

7.1.4.1 Positional Sanctification

Positional sanctification refers to the believer's status as holy, set apart by God at the moment of salvation. 1 Corinthians 1:2 addresses believers as "those sanctified in Christ Jesus and called to be His holy people." This sanctification is a definitive act of God, establishing the believer's identity in Christ.

7.1.4.2 Progressive Sanctification

Progressive sanctification is the ongoing process of spiritual growth and transformation. Philippians 2:12-13 exhorts believers to "continue to work out your salvation with fear and trembling, for it is God who works in you to will and to act in order to fulfill His good purpose." This process involves the believer's active cooperation with the Holy Spirit, who empowers them to live a life of holiness.

7.1.4.3 Means of Sanctification

Sanctification is accomplished through various means, including the Word of God, prayer, fellowship, and the sacraments. John 17:17 emphasizes the role of Scripture: "Sanctify them by the truth; your word is truth." The Holy Spirit uses these means to transform the believer's character and conduct.

7.1.5 Glorification

Glorification is the final stage of salvation, where believers are perfected in holiness and enjoy eternal life in God's presence. It involves the resurrection of the body and the full realization of God's redemptive purposes.

7.1.5.1 Resurrection of the Body

The resurrection of the body is a key aspect of glorification. 1 Corinthians 15:42-44 explains, "So will it be with the resurrection of the dead. The body that is sown is perishable, it is raised imperishable; it is sown in dishonor, it is raised in glory; it is sown in weakness, it is raised in power; it is sown a natural body, it is raised a spiritual body." Believers will receive glorified bodies, free from sin and death.

7.1.5.2 Eternal Life

Glorification includes the enjoyment of eternal life in God's presence. Revelation 21:3-4 describes this glorious future: "And I heard a loud voice from the throne saying,

'Look! God's dwelling place is now among the people, and He will dwell with them. They will be His people, and God Himself will be with them and be their God. He will wipe every tear from their eyes. There will be no more death or mourning or crying or pain, for the old order of things has passed away." This eternal state signifies the fulfillment of God's redemptive plan and the consummation of His kingdom.

7.1.5.3 Assurance of Glorification

The assurance of glorification is grounded in God's faithfulness. Romans 8:30 concludes, "And those He predestined, He also called; those He called, He also justified; those He justified, He also glorified." This unbreakable chain of salvation guarantees that God will bring His work to completion.

7.1.6 Practical Implications of the Plan of Salvation

Understanding God's plan of salvation has significant practical implications for believers, shaping their identity, purpose, and daily living.

7.1.6.1 Assurance of Salvation

Believers can have assurance of their salvation, knowing that it is rooted in God's eternal plan and accomplished through Christ's work. John 10:28-29 provides this assurance: "I give them eternal life, and they shall never perish; no one will snatch them out of my hand. My Father, who has given them to me, is greater than all; no one can snatch them out of my Father's hand." This assurance fosters confidence and security in the believer's relationship with God.

7.1.6.2 Motivation for Holiness

The knowledge of God's plan motivates believers to pursue holiness. 1 Peter 1:15-16 exhorts, "But just as He who called you is holy, so be holy in all you do; for it is written: 'Be holy because I am holy.'" Recognizing that sanctification is part of God's plan encourages believers to live in accordance with their new identity in Christ.

7.1.6.3 Commitment to Mission

Believers are called to participate in God's redemptive mission by proclaiming the gospel and making disciples. Matthew 28:19-20 commissions, "Therefore go and make disciples of all nations, baptizing them in the name of the Father and of the Son and of the Holy Spirit, and teaching them to obey everything I have commanded you. And surely I am with you always, to the very end of the age." Understanding God's plan inspires commitment to evangelism and discipleship.

7.1.6.4 Hope and Perseverance

The promise of glorification provides hope and perseverance in the face of trials and suffering. Romans 8:18 offers this perspective: "I consider that our present sufferings are not worth comparing with the glory that will be revealed in us." This hope enables believers to endure hardships with the assurance of future glory.

7.1.7 Conclusion

The plan of salvation is a comprehensive framework that reflects God's eternal purpose and redemptive work. It involves the calling, justification, sanctification, and glorification of believers, highlighting the transformative power of Christ's work and the assurance of God's promises. Understanding this plan shapes believers' identity, motivates holiness, inspires mission, and provides hope in the face of suffering. As we continue to explore systematic theology, the doctrine of salvation remains central to our understanding of God's grace and His plan for humanity.

7.2 Justification

Justification is a foundational doctrine of the Christian faith, representing the act of God whereby He declares sinners to be righteous based on the righteousness of Christ. This declaration is made possible through the atoning work of Jesus and is received by faith alone, apart from works. Understanding justification is crucial for comprehending the nature of salvation, the role of faith, and the assurance of a right relationship with God. In this chapter, we will explore the biblical basis, theological significance, and practical implications of justification.

7.2.1 Biblical Basis of Justification

The doctrine of justification is rooted in Scripture, with key passages in both the Old and New Testaments providing a comprehensive understanding of this essential truth.

7.2.1.1 Justification in the Old Testament

While the term "justification" is more fully developed in the New Testament, the concept is present in the Old Testament. Genesis 15:6 states, "Abram believed the Lord, and He credited it to him as righteousness." This verse highlights the principle that righteousness is credited to those who have faith in God.

The prophetic books also point to justification. Isaiah 53:11 speaks of the suffering servant, who "by His knowledge, my righteous servant will justify many, and He will bear their iniquities." This passage foreshadows the work of Christ in justifying sinners.

7.2.1.2 Justification in the New Testament

The New Testament provides a fuller revelation of justification, particularly through the writings of the Apostle

Paul. Romans 3:28 states, "For we maintain that a person is justified by faith apart from the works of the law." This verse succinctly captures the essence of justification by faith alone.

Romans 5:1-2 further explains, "Therefore, since we have been justified through faith, we have peace with God through our Lord Jesus Christ, through whom we have gained access by faith into this grace in which we now stand." Justification brings peace with God and access to His grace.

Galatians 2:16 emphasizes the distinction between faith and works: "know that a person is not justified by the works of the law, but by faith in Jesus Christ. So we, too, have put our faith in Christ Jesus that we may be justified by faith in Christ and not by the works of the law because by the works of the law, no one will be justified."

7.2.2 Theological Significance of Justification

Justification is a central tenet of Christian theology, with profound implications for understanding the nature of salvation, the role of faith, and the relationship between grace and works.

7.2.2.1 Imputation of Righteousness

Justification involves the imputation of Christ's righteousness to the believer. 2 Corinthians 5:21 explains, "God made Him who had no sin to be sin for us, so that in Him we might become the righteousness of God." This imputation means that Christ's perfect obedience and sacrificial death are credited to the believer's account, enabling them to stand righteous before God.

7.2.2.2 Forensic Declaration

Justification is a forensic, or legal, declaration. It does not mean that the believer is made righteous in their behavior immediately but that they are declared righteous in God's sight. Romans 8:33-34 affirms, "Who will bring any charge against those whom God has chosen? It is God who justifies. Who then is the one who condemns? No one. Christ Jesus who died—more than that, who was raised to life—is at the right hand of God and is also interceding for us." This legal declaration removes any basis for condemnation.

7.2.2.3 By Faith Alone

The principle of justification by faith alone (sola fide) is central to the doctrine. Ephesians 2:8-9 clarifies, "For it is by grace you have been saved, through faith—and this is not from yourselves, it is the gift of God—not by works so that no one can boast." Faith is the means by which believers receive the gift of justification, excluding any reliance on human merit or works.

7.2.2.4 Grace and Works

Justification underscores the relationship between grace and works. While justification is received by faith alone, genuine faith produces works as evidence of salvation. James 2:17 states, "In the same way, faith by itself, if it is not accompanied by action, is dead." Works are not the basis of justification but the fruit of a living faith.

7.2.3 Practical Implications of Justification

The doctrine of justification has significant practical implications for the believer's assurance, spiritual life, and ethical conduct.

7.2.3.1 Assurance of Salvation

Justification provides the believer with assurance of salvation. Romans 5:1 states, "Therefore, since we have been justified through faith, we have peace with God through our Lord Jesus Christ." This peace with God offers confidence and security in the believer's relationship with Him, knowing that their standing is based on Christ's righteousness and not their own efforts.

7.2.3.2 Freedom from Guilt and Condemnation

Justification liberates the believer from guilt and condemnation. Romans 8:1 declares, "Therefore, there is now no condemnation for those who are in Christ Jesus." This freedom allows believers to live in the joy and liberty of God's grace, without the burden of past sins.

7.2.3.3 Motivation for Holy Living

Understanding justification motivates believers to pursue holy living. While justification is by faith alone, it leads to sanctification—a process of growing in holiness. Titus 2:11-12 teaches, "For the grace of God has appeared that offers salvation to all people. It teaches us to say 'No' to ungodliness and worldly passions, and to live self-controlled, upright, and godly lives in this present age." The grace that justifies also sanctifies, empowering believers to live in a manner worthy of their calling.

7.2.3.4 Encouragement in Evangelism

The doctrine of justification encourages evangelism. Knowing that salvation is a gift of God's grace received by faith, believers are motivated to share the gospel with others. Romans 10:13-15 highlights the importance of proclaiming the message: "for, 'Everyone who calls on the name of the Lord will be saved.' How, then, can they call on the one they have not believed in? And how can they believe in the one of whom they have not heard? And how can they hear without someone preaching to them? And how can anyone preach unless they are sent? As it is written: 'How beautiful are the feet of those who bring good news!'"

7.2.3.5 Unity and Fellowship

Justification fosters unity and fellowship within the body of Christ. Ephesians 2:14-16 states, "For He Himself is our peace, who has made the two groups one and has destroyed the barrier, the dividing wall of hostility, by setting aside in His flesh the law with its commands and regulations. His purpose was to create in Himself one new humanity out of the two, thus making peace, and in one body to reconcile both of them to God through the cross, by which He put to death their hostility." The doctrine of justification breaks down barriers and unites believers in the common bond of grace.

7.2.4 Common Misunderstandings of Justification

While the doctrine of justification is foundational, it is often misunderstood or misrepresented. Addressing these misconceptions is essential for a clear understanding of the gospel.

7.2.4.1 Justification and Sanctification Confusion

One common misunderstanding is confusing justification with sanctification. Justification is a one-time legal declaration of righteousness, while sanctification is the ongoing process of becoming holy. Philippians 3:9 clarifies this distinction: "and be found in Him, not having a righteousness of my own that comes from the law, but that which is through faith in Christ—the righteousness that comes from God on the basis of faith."

7.2.4.2 Legalism

Legalism is the belief that one can earn justification through adherence to the law or good works. Galatians 2:16 refutes this notion: "know that a person is not justified by the works of the law, but by faith in Jesus Christ. So we, too, have put our faith in Christ Jesus that we may be justified by faith in Christ and not by the works of the law because by the works of the law, no one will be justified."

7.2.4.3 Antinomianism

Antinomianism is the belief that, because of grace, believers are not bound to follow moral laws. This view neglects the transformative power of grace that leads to holy living. Romans 6:1-2 addresses this error: "What shall we say, then? Shall we go on sinning so that grace may increase? By no means! We are those who have died to sin; how can we live in it any longer?"

7.2.5 Conclusion

Justification is a fundamental doctrine of the Christian faith, emphasizing that sinners are declared righteous based on the righteousness of Christ, received by faith alone. This legal declaration by God provides assurance of salvation, freedom from guilt, motivation for holy living, encouragement in evangelism, and unity within the body of Christ. Understanding and embracing the doctrine of justification enables believers to live in the joy and liberty of God's grace, fully assured of their standing before Him.

As we continue to explore systematic theology, the doctrine of justification remains central to our understanding of God's redemptive work and the transformative power of the gospel.

7.3 Sanctification

Sanctification is the process by which believers are progressively transformed into the image of Christ. It involves both divine initiative and human responsibility, as God works in believers to produce holiness and righteousness, and believers actively cooperate with this transformative process. Sanctification is a vital aspect of the Christian life, emphasizing growth in spiritual maturity and conformity to the character of Christ. In this chapter, we will explore the biblical basis, theological significance, and practical implications of sanctification.

7.3.1 Biblical Basis of Sanctification

The doctrine of sanctification is deeply rooted in Scripture, with numerous passages highlighting its importance and outlining its process.

7.3.1.1 Positional Sanctification

Positional sanctification refers to the believer's status as holy, set apart by God at the moment of conversion. 1

Corinthians 1:2 addresses believers as "those sanctified in Christ Jesus and called to be His holy people." This sanctification is a definitive act of God, establishing the believer's identity in Christ.

7.3.1.2 Progressive Sanctification

Progressive sanctification is the ongoing process of spiritual growth and transformation that continues throughout the believer's life. Philippians 2:12-13 captures this dual aspect: "Therefore, my dear friends, as you have always obeyed—not only in my presence but now much more in my absence—continue to work out your salvation with fear and trembling, for it is God who works in you to will and to act in order to fulfill His good purpose." Believers are called to actively pursue holiness while relying on God's power.

7.3.1.3 Ultimate Sanctification

Ultimate sanctification refers to the final perfection of believers when they are fully conformed to the image of Christ. 1 John 3:2 promises, "Dear friends, now we are children of God, and what we will be has not yet been made known. But we know that when Christ appears, we shall be like Him, for we shall see Him as He is." This future aspect of sanctification assures believers of complete transformation in the presence of God.

7.3.2 Theological Significance of Sanctification

Sanctification is crucial for understanding the believer's growth in holiness and the transformative work of the Holy Spirit.

7.3.2.1 Holiness and Purity

Sanctification involves the pursuit of holiness and purity. 1 Peter 1:15-16 exhorts, "But just as He who called you is holy, so be holy in all you do; for it is written: 'Be holy, because I am holy.'" Holiness is both a positional reality and a practical goal, reflecting God's character and moral perfection.

7.3.2.2 Conformity to Christ

The goal of sanctification is conformity to the image of Christ. Romans 8:29 explains, "For those God foreknew He also predestined to be conformed to the image of His Son, that He might be the firstborn among many brothers and sisters." This conformity involves growing in Christlike character, attitudes, and actions.

7.3.2.3 The Role of the Holy Spirit

The Holy Spirit plays a central role in sanctification, empowering and guiding believers in their spiritual growth. Galatians 5:16 states, "So I say, walk by the Spirit, and you will not gratify the desires of the flesh." The Spirit's work involves producing the fruit of the Spirit in believers' lives, transforming them from within.

7.3.3 Means of Sanctification

Sanctification is facilitated through various means that God has provided for spiritual growth and maturity.

7.3.3.1 The Word of God

The Word of God is a primary means of sanctification. John 17:17 emphasizes, "Sanctify them by the truth; your word is truth." Scripture instructs, corrects, and equips believers for righteous living, providing the foundation for spiritual growth.

7.3.3.2 Prayer

Prayer is essential for sanctification, enabling believers to commune with God, seek His guidance, and receive His strength. Philippians 4:6-7 encourages, "Do not be anxious about anything, but in every situation, by prayer and petition, with thanksgiving, present your requests to God. And the peace of God, which transcends all understanding, will guard your hearts and your minds in Christ Jesus."

7.3.3.3 Fellowship

Fellowship with other believers supports sanctification by providing encouragement, accountability, and mutual edification. Hebrews 10:24-25 advises, "And let us consider how we may spur one another on toward love and good deeds, not giving up meeting together, as some are in the habit of doing, but encouraging one another—and all the more as you see the Day approaching."

7.3.3.4 Sacraments

The sacraments, such as baptism and the Lord's Supper, are means of grace that strengthen faith and promote spiritual growth. 1 Corinthians 11:26 speaks of the Lord's Supper: "For whenever you eat this bread and drink this cup, you proclaim the Lord's death until He comes." These practices remind believers of their identity in Christ and their dependence on His redemptive work.

7.3.4 Human Responsibility in Sanctification

While sanctification is primarily the work of God, believers are called to actively participate in the process through obedience, discipline, and effort.

7.3.4.1 Obedience to God's Commands

Believers are called to obey God's commands as an expression of their sanctification. John 14:15 states, "If you love me, keep my commands." Obedience demonstrates love for God and commitment to His will.

7.3.4.2 Spiritual Disciplines

Engaging in spiritual disciplines, such as Bible study, prayer, fasting, and worship, cultivates growth in holiness. 1 Timothy 4:7 exhorts, "Have nothing to do with godless myths and old wives' tales; rather, train yourself to be godly."

Discipline and intentionality are crucial for spiritual development.

7.3.4.3 Resisting Temptation

Resisting temptation is a vital aspect of sanctification. James 4:7 advises, "Submit yourselves, then, to God. Resist the devil, and he will flee from you." Believers must rely on God's strength to overcome sinful desires and actions.

7.3.5 Practical Implications of Sanctification

Sanctification has significant practical implications for the believer's daily life, relationships, and mission.

7.3.5.1 Personal Holiness

Sanctification calls believers to personal holiness, impacting their thoughts, words, and actions. 2 Corinthians 7:1 urges, "Therefore, since we have these promises, dear friends, let us purify ourselves from everything that contaminates body and spirit, perfecting holiness out of reverence for God." Pursuing holiness involves rejecting sinful behaviors and cultivating godly virtues.

7.3.5.2 Relational Harmony

Sanctification fosters relational harmony within the body of Christ. Ephesians 4:1-3 emphasizes, "As a prisoner for the Lord, then, I urge you to live a life worthy of the calling you have received. Be completely humble and gentle; be patient, bearing with one another in love. Make every effort to keep the unity of the Spirit through the bond of peace." Growing in Christlikeness enhances relationships and promotes unity.

7.3.5.3 Witness to the World

Sanctification enhances the believer's witness to the world. Matthew 5:16 encourages, "In the same way, let your light shine before others, that they may see your good deeds and glorify your Father in heaven." A transformed life reflects the power of the gospel and draws others to Christ.

7.3.5.4 Endurance in Trials

Sanctification provides strength and endurance in the face of trials and suffering. Romans 5:3-4 teaches, "Not only so, but we also glory in our sufferings because we know that suffering produces perseverance; perseverance, character; and character, hope." Through sanctification, believers develop resilience and hope, trusting in God's faithfulness.

7.3.6 Conclusion

Sanctification is a dynamic and ongoing process by which believers are progressively transformed into the image of Christ. It involves both divine initiative and human responsibility, as God works in believers to produce holiness and righteousness, and believers actively cooperate with this transformative process. Understanding sanctification is crucial for spiritual growth, personal holiness, and effective witness.

Through the means of sanctification provided by God, such as the Word, prayer, fellowship, and the sacraments, believers are empowered to grow in Christlikeness and fulfill their calling. As we continue to explore systematic theology, the doctrine of sanctification remains central to our understanding of the Christian life and the pursuit of holiness.

7.4 Glorification

Glorification is the final stage of salvation, the culmination of God's redemptive plan where believers are fully conformed to the image of Christ and enjoy eternal life with God. This doctrine is crucial for understanding the ultimate hope and destiny of believers. Glorification involves the resurrection of the body, the eradication of sin, and the eternal fellowship with God. In this chapter, we will explore the biblical basis, theological significance, and practical implications of glorification.

7.4.1 Biblical Basis of Glorification

The concept of glorification is deeply rooted in Scripture, providing a future-oriented perspective on salvation and eternal life.

7.4.1.1 Romans 8:30

Romans 8:30 succinctly outlines the process of salvation, culminating in glorification: "And those He predestined, He also called; those He called, He also justified; those He justified, He also glorified." This verse highlights the certainty of glorification for those who are in Christ, affirming it as the final step in the salvation process.

7.4.1.2 The Resurrection of the Body

The resurrection of the body is a central aspect of glorification. 1 Corinthians 15:42-44 describes this transformation: "So will it be with the resurrection of the dead. The body that is sown is perishable, it is raised imperishable; it is sown in dishonor, it is raised in glory; it is sown in weakness, it is raised in power; it is sown a natural body, it is raised a spiritual body." Believers will receive glorified bodies that are imperishable, powerful, and spiritual.

7.4.1.3 Eternal Life with God

Glorification ensures eternal life with God. Revelation 21:3-4 provides a vivid picture of this eternal state: "And I heard a loud voice from the throne saying, 'Look! God's dwelling place is now among the people, and He will dwell with them. They will be His people, and God Himself will be with them and be their God. He will wipe every tear from their eyes. There will be no more death' or mourning or crying or pain, for the old order of things has passed away.'" This passage emphasizes the intimate fellowship believers will enjoy with God, free from sorrow and death.

7.4.2 Theological Significance of Glorification

Glorification is significant for understanding the culmination of God's redemptive work and the believer's ultimate destiny.

7.4.2.1 Full Conformity to Christ

Glorification involves full conformity to the image of Christ. Philippians 3:20-21 states, "But our citizenship is in heaven. And we eagerly await a Savior from there, the Lord Jesus Christ, who, by the power that enables Him to bring everything under His control, will transform our lowly bodies so that they will be like His glorious body." This transformation ensures that believers will perfectly reflect Christ's character and glory.

7.4.2.2 Completion of Salvation

Glorification marks the completion of salvation. Hebrews 12:23 refers to "the spirits of the righteous made perfect," indicating that believers will be made completely holy and righteous. This final step in salvation eradicates all remnants of sin and its effects.

7.4.2.3 Participation in Divine Glory

Believers will participate in divine glory. 2 Peter 1:3-4 explains, "His divine power has given us everything we need for a godly life through our knowledge of Him who called us by His own glory and goodness. Through these He has given us His very great and precious promises, so that through them you may participate in the divine nature, having escaped the corruption in the world caused by evil desires." This participation in the divine nature signifies a profound transformation and fellowship with God.

7.4.3 The Process of Glorification

Glorification involves several key elements that outline the process and experience of this final stage of salvation.

7.4.3.1 Resurrection of the Dead

The resurrection of the dead is a fundamental aspect of glorification. 1 Thessalonians 4:16-17 describes this event: "For the Lord Himself will come down from heaven, with a loud command, with the voice of the archangel and with the trumpet call of God, and the dead in Christ will rise first. After that, we who are still alive and are left will be caught up together with them in the clouds to meet the Lord in the air. And so we will be with the Lord forever." This resurrection reunites believers with Christ in a transformed state.

7.4.3.2 Transformation of the Living

Believers who are alive at Christ's return will also be transformed. 1 Corinthians 15:51-52 states, "Listen, I tell you a mystery: We will not all sleep, but we will all be changed—in a flash, in the twinkling of an eye, at the last trumpet. For the trumpet will sound, the dead will be raised imperishable, and we will be changed." This transformation ensures that all believers, whether dead or alive, will experience glorification.

7.4.3.3 Eradication of Sin and Death

Glorification includes the complete eradication of sin and death. Revelation 21:4 emphasizes, "He will wipe every tear from their eyes. There will be no more death' or mourning or crying or pain, for the old order of things has passed away." The new creation will be free from the effects of sin, resulting in perfect peace and joy.

7.4.4 Practical Implications of Glorification

Understanding glorification has profound practical implications for the believer's life, providing hope, motivation, and a perspective on suffering and mission.

7.4.4.1 Hope and Assurance

Glorification provides believers with hope and assurance. Romans 8:18 states, "I consider that our present sufferings are not worth comparing with the glory that will be revealed in us." This future glory gives believers confidence and hope, enabling them to endure present trials with the assurance of a glorious future.

7.4.4.2 Motivation for Holiness

The promise of glorification motivates believers to pursue holiness. 1 John 3:2-3 encourages, "Dear friends, now we are children of God, and what we will be has not yet been made known. But we know that when Christ appears, we shall be like Him, for we shall see Him as He is. All who have this hope in Him purify themselves, just as He is pure." Knowing that they will be fully conformed to Christ's image inspires believers to strive for purity and godliness in their current lives.

7.4.4.3 Perspective on Suffering

Glorification offers a perspective on suffering, viewing it in light of eternal glory. 2 Corinthians 4:17-18 explains, "For our light and momentary troubles are achieving for us an eternal glory that far outweighs them all. So we fix our eyes not on what is seen, but on what is unseen since what is seen is temporary, but what is unseen is eternal." This perspective helps believers endure suffering with the knowledge that it contributes to their future glory.

7.4.4.4 Encouragement in Mission

The doctrine of glorification encourages believers to participate in God's mission. Matthew 24:14 promises, "And this gospel of the kingdom will be preached in the whole world as a testimony to all nations, and then the end will come." Understanding the ultimate goal of glorification motivates believers to spread the gospel, inviting others to share in this future glory.

7.4.5 Conclusion

Glorification is the final stage of salvation, where believers are fully conformed to the image of Christ and enjoy eternal life with God. This doctrine is essential for understanding the culmination of God's redemptive work and the ultimate hope and destiny of believers. Through the resurrection of the body, the eradication of sin, and eternal fellowship with God, glorification provides a comprehensive vision of the believer's future.

Understanding glorification shapes the believer's present life, providing hope, motivation for holiness, perspective on suffering, and encouragement in mission. As we continue to explore systematic theology, the doctrine of glorification remains central to our understanding of God's ultimate purpose for humanity and the fulfillment of His redemptive plan.

CHAPTER 08

THE NATURE OF THE CHURCH

8.1 The Nature of the Church

The doctrine of the church, or ecclesiology, is a vital aspect of Christian theology, examining the nature, purpose, and mission of the church as the body of Christ. Understanding the nature of the church is crucial for grasping its role in God's redemptive plan and the believer's place within the community of faith. The church is described in Scripture with various metaphors, such as the body of Christ, the bride of Christ, and the temple of the Holy Spirit. In this chapter, we will explore these biblical descriptions, their theological significance, and their practical implications.

8.1.1 The Church as the Body of Christ

One of the most profound images of the church in the New Testament is the body of Christ. This metaphor emphasizes the unity, diversity, and interdependence of believers, as well as the church's connection to Christ as its head.

8.1.1.1 Unity and Diversity

The metaphor of the body highlights both the unity and diversity of the church. 1 Corinthians 12:12-13 explains, "Just as a body, though one, has many parts, but all its many parts form one body, so it is with Christ. For we were all baptized by one Spirit so as to form one body—whether Jews or Gentiles, slave or free—and we were all given the one Spirit to drink." This passage underscores that all believers, regardless of their backgrounds, are united in Christ and form one body.

8.1.1.2 Interdependence

The body metaphor also emphasizes the interdependence of believers. Each member has a unique role and function, contributing to the health and growth of the whole body. 1 Corinthians 12:21-22 states, "The eye cannot say to the hand, 'I don't need you!' And the head cannot say to the feet, 'I don't need you!' On the contrary, those parts of the body that seem to be weaker are indispensable." This interdependence fosters mutual care and cooperation within the church.

8.1.1.3 Christ as the Head

Christ is the head of the body, providing leadership, direction, and sustenance. Ephesians 1:22-23 affirms, "And God placed all things under His feet and appointed Him to be head over everything for the church, which is His body, the fullness of Him who fills everything in every way." This relationship underscores the church's dependence on Christ and its calling to reflect His character and mission.

8.1.2 The Church as the Bride of Christ

The metaphor of the church as the bride of Christ highlights the intimate and covenantal relationship between Christ and His people. This imagery conveys love, fidelity, and the eschatological hope of union with Christ.

8.1.2.1 Covenant Relationship

The image of the bride reflects the church's covenant relationship with Christ. Ephesians 5:25-27 compares Christ's love for the church to that of a husband for his wife: "Husbands, love your wives, just as Christ loved the church and gave Himself up for her to make her holy, cleansing her by the washing with water through the word, and to present her to Himself as a radiant church, without stain or wrinkle or any other blemish, but holy and blameless." This covenant relationship is founded on Christ's sacrificial love and commitment.

8.1.2.2 Purity and Holiness

As the bride of Christ, the church is called to purity and holiness. Revelation 19:7-8 speaks of the marriage supper of the Lamb: "Let us rejoice and be glad and give Him glory! For the wedding of the Lamb has come, and His bride has made herself ready. Fine linen, bright and clean, was given her to wear." The church's purity is a reflection of its sanctification and preparation for eternal union with Christ.

8.1.2.3 Eschatological Hope

The metaphor of the bride also conveys the eschatological hope of the church's future union with Christ. Revelation 21:2 describes the New Jerusalem as "a bride beautifully dressed for her husband." This future reality motivates the church to live in faithful anticipation of Christ's return and the consummation of God's redemptive plan.

8.1.3 The Church as the Temple of the Holy Spirit

The image of the church as the temple of the Holy Spirit emphasizes the indwelling presence of God and the calling of the church to be a holy community.

8.1.3.1 Indwelling Presence

The church is described as the dwelling place of God through the Spirit. 1 Corinthians 3:16 states, "Don't you know that you yourselves are God's temple and that God's Spirit dwells in your midst?" This indwelling presence signifies the church's identity as a community where God resides and manifests His presence.

8.1.3.2 Holiness and Sanctification

As the temple of the Holy Spirit, the church is called to holiness and sanctification. 1 Peter 2:5 describes believers as "living stones" being built into a spiritual house: "You also, like living stones, are being built into a spiritual house to be a holy priesthood, offering spiritual sacrifices acceptable to God through Jesus Christ." This calling involves living in a manner that reflects God's holiness and purity.

8.1.3.3 Worship and Service

The church, as the temple of the Holy Spirit, is a place of worship and service. Ephesians 2:21-22 explains, "In Him, the whole building is joined together and rises to become a holy temple in the Lord. And in Him, you too are being built together to become a dwelling in which God lives by His Spirit." Worship and service are central to the church's identity and mission, expressing the community's devotion to God and its commitment to serving others.

8.1.4 Practical Implications of the Nature of the Church

Understanding the nature of the church has significant practical implications for the life and mission of the community of believers.

8.1.4.1 Unity and Diversity

The church's nature as the body of Christ calls for unity and appreciation of diversity. Ephesians 4:3-6 exhorts believers to "make every effort to keep the unity of the Spirit through the bond of peace. There is one body and one Spirit, just as you were called to one hope when you were called; one Lord, one faith, one baptism; one God and Father of all, who is over all and through all and in all." This unity is grounded in shared faith and the indwelling Spirit, while diversity is celebrated as each member contributes unique gifts and perspectives.

8.1.4.2 Mutual Care and Support

The interdependence of the body of Christ emphasizes the importance of mutual care and support. Galatians 6:2 instructs, "Carry each other's burdens, and in this way you will fulfill the law of Christ." The church is called to care for one another, providing encouragement, support, and practical assistance.

8.1.4.3 Commitment to Holiness

The church's identity as the bride of Christ and the temple of the Holy Spirit calls for a commitment to holiness. 1 Thessalonians 4:7 reminds believers, "For God did not call us to be impure, but to live a holy life." This commitment involves personal and communal sanctification, reflecting the church's calling to be a holy community.

8.1.4.4 Active Participation in Worship and Service

As the temple of the Holy Spirit, the church is a community of worship and service. Romans 12:1 urges believers, "Therefore, I urge you, brothers and sisters, in view of God's mercy, to offer your bodies as a living sacrifice, holy and pleasing to God—this is your true and proper worship." Active participation in worship and service is a response to God's grace and an expression of the church's mission.

8.1.4.5 Hope and Anticipation

The church's eschatological hope as the bride of Christ motivates believers to live in anticipation of Christ's return. Titus 2:13 encourages, "while we wait for the blessed hope—the appearing of the glory of our great God and Savior, Jesus Christ." This hope inspires faithful living and active engagement in God's redemptive mission.

8.1.5 Conclusion

The nature of the church is a multifaceted and profound doctrine that reveals the church's identity, purpose, and mission. Described as the body of Christ, the bride of Christ, and the temple of the Holy Spirit, the church is a community of all true believers in Christ, united in faith, diverse in gifts, and called to holiness and service.

Understanding these biblical metaphors enriches the church's self-understanding and informs its practice, fostering unity, mutual care, commitment to holiness, active worship, and hope. As we continue to explore systematic theology, the doctrine of the church remains central to our understanding of God's redemptive plan and the believer's role within the community of faith.

8.2 The Purpose of the Church

The doctrine of the church, or ecclesiology, not only examines the nature of the church but also its purpose. Understanding the purpose of the church is crucial for comprehending its role in God's redemptive plan and its mission in the world. The church exists to worship God, edify believers, and evangelize the world. It is called to be a witness to God's grace and truth. In this chapter, we will explore these purposes, their biblical basis, and their practical implications.

8.2.1 Worship

Worship is the primary purpose of the church. The church exists to glorify God, recognizing Him as the Creator and Redeemer, and offering Him praise, adoration, and thanksgiving.

8.2.1.1 Biblical Basis for Worship

Worship is central to the life of the church. Acts 2:42-47 describes the early church's commitment to worship:

"They devoted themselves to the apostles' teaching and to fellowship, to the breaking of bread and to prayer. ... They broke bread in their homes and ate together with glad and sincere hearts, praising God and enjoying the favor of all the people." This passage highlights the church's dedication to teaching, fellowship, the Lord's Supper, and prayer, all of which are acts of worship.

John 4:23-24 emphasizes the importance of worshiping in spirit and truth: "Yet a time is coming and has now come when the true worshipers will worship the Father in the Spirit and in truth, for they are the kind of worshipers the Father seeks. God is spirit, and His worshipers must worship in the Spirit and in truth."

8.2.1.2 Theological Significance of Worship

Worship is the proper response to God's revelation of Himself. Romans 11:36 states, "For from Him and through Him and for Him are all things. To Him be the glory forever! Amen." Worship acknowledges God's sovereignty, holiness, and love, and it draws the church into a deeper relationship with Him.

8.2.1.3 Practical Implications of Worship

- Corporate Worship: The church gathers regularly for corporate worship, which includes singing, prayer, preaching, and the sacraments. Hebrews 10:25 encourages, "not giving up meeting together, as some are in the habit of doing, but encouraging one another—and all the more as you see the Day approaching."

- Personal Worship: Worship is also a personal practice, as believers are called to live lives of continual worship. Romans 12:1 urges, "Therefore, I urge you, brothers and sisters, in view of God's mercy, to offer your bodies as a living sacrifice, holy and pleasing to God—this is your true and proper worship."

- Lifestyle of Worship: Worship extends beyond formal gatherings to encompass all of life. Colossians 3:17 instructs, "And whatever you do, whether in word or deed, do it all in the name of the Lord Jesus, giving thanks to God the Father through Him."

8.2.2 Edification

The edification of believers is another primary purpose of the church. Edification involves building up the body of Christ through teaching, discipleship, fellowship, and mutual encouragement.

8.2.2.1 Biblical Basis for Edification

Ephesians 4:11-13 outlines the role of church leaders in edifying the body of Christ: "So Christ Himself gave the apostles, the prophets, the evangelists, the pastors and teachers, to equip His people for works of service, so that the body of Christ may be built up until we all reach unity in the faith and in the knowledge of the Son of God and become mature, attaining to the whole measure of the fullness of Christ." This passage emphasizes the goal of edification as maturity in faith and unity in Christ.

Acts 2:42-47 also reflects the early church's commitment to edification through teaching and fellowship.

8.2.2.2 Theological Significance of Edification

Edification is essential for the spiritual growth and maturity of believers. 1 Corinthians 14:12 encourages the church to "try to excel in those that build up the church." Edification strengthens the faith of believers, promotes unity, and prepares them for effective ministry.

8.2.2.3 Practical Implications of Edification

- Teaching and Preaching: Sound teaching and preaching are crucial for edification. 2 Timothy 4:2 urges, "Preach the word; be prepared in season and out of season; correct, rebuke and encourage—with great patience and careful instruction."

- Discipleship: Discipleship involves mentoring and guiding believers toward spiritual maturity. Matthew 28:19-20 commands, "Therefore go and make disciples of all nations, baptizing them in the name of the Father and of the Son and of the Holy Spirit, and teaching them to obey everything I have commanded you."

- Fellowship and Community: Fellowship and community life are vital for mutual edification. Hebrews 10:24-25 advises, "And let us consider how we may spur one another on toward love and good deeds, not giving up meeting together, as some are in the habit of doing, but encouraging one another—and all the more as you see the Day approaching."

- Spiritual Gifts: The exercise of spiritual gifts builds up the church. 1 Corinthians 12:7 states, "Now to each one the manifestation of the Spirit is given for the common good." Believers are called to use their gifts to serve one another and promote spiritual growth.

8.2.3 Evangelism

Evangelism is a fundamental purpose of the church, involving the proclamation of the gospel to the world. The church is called to bear witness to God's grace and truth, inviting others to faith in Christ.

8.2.3.1 Biblical Basis for Evangelism

The Great Commission in Matthew 28:18-20 provides the foundation for evangelism: "Then Jesus came to them and said, 'All authority in heaven and on earth has been given to me. Therefore go and make disciples of all nations, baptizing them in the name of the Father and of the Son and of the Holy Spirit, and teaching them to obey everything I have commanded you. And surely I am with you always, to the very end of the age.'" This command underscores the church's mission to spread the gospel and make disciples.

Acts 1:8 further emphasizes the church's role in evangelism: "But you will receive power when the Holy Spirit comes on you, and you will be my witnesses in Jerusalem, and in all Judea and Samaria, and to the ends of the earth."

8.2.3.2 Theological Significance of Evangelism

Evangelism reflects God's desire for all people to come to repentance and faith. 1 Timothy 2:3-4 states, "This is good, and pleases God our Savior, who wants all people to be saved and to come to a knowledge of the truth." Evangelism is a response to God's love and participation in His redemptive mission.

8.2.3.3 Practical Implications of Evangelism

- Proclamation of the Gospel: Evangelism involves proclaiming the gospel message. Romans 10:14-15 asks, "How, then, can they call on the one they have not believed in? And how can they believe in the one of whom they have not heard? And how can they hear without someone preaching to them? And how can anyone preach unless they are sent? As it is written: 'How beautiful are the feet of those who bring good news!'"

- Personal Witness: Every believer is called to be a witness to Christ. 1 Peter 3:15 encourages, "But in your hearts revere Christ as Lord. Always be prepared to give an answer to everyone who asks you to give the reason for the hope that you have. But do this with gentleness and respect."

- Community Outreach: The church engages in community outreach to meet needs and share the gospel. Matthew 5:16 instructs, "In the same way, let your light shine before others, that they may see your good deeds and glorify your Father in heaven."

- Global Missions: The church is called to participate in global missions, spreading the gospel to all nations. Acts 13:47 declares, "For this is what the Lord has commanded us: 'I have made you a light for the Gentiles, that you may bring salvation to the ends of the earth.'"

8.2.4 The Church as a Witness

The church is called to be a witness to God's grace and truth, reflecting His character and proclaiming His message to the world.

8.2.4.1 Biblical Basis for Witness

Acts 1:8 provides the foundation for the church's witness: "But you will receive power when the Holy Spirit comes on you; and you will be my witnesses in Jerusalem, and in all Judea and Samaria, and to the ends of the earth." The church's witness is empowered by the Holy Spirit and extends to all the earth.

8.2.4.2 Theological Significance of Witness

The church's witness reflects God's mission to reveal Himself and His salvation to the world. John 17:18 states, "As you sent me into the world, I have sent them into the world." The church participates in Christ's mission by bearing witness to His life, death, and resurrection.

8.2.4.3 Practical Implications of Witness

- Authentic Living: The church's witness involves authentic living that reflects God's character. Matthew 5:14-16 emphasizes, "You are the light of

the world. A town built on a hill cannot be hidden. Neither do people light a lamp and put it under a bowl. Instead, they put it on its stand, and it gives light to everyone in the house. In the same way, let your light shine before others, that they may see your good deeds and glorify your Father in heaven."

- Proclamation of Truth: The church is called to proclaim God's truth in a world of relativism and falsehood. Ephesians 4:15 advises, "Instead, speaking the truth in love, we will grow to become in every respect the mature body of Him who is the head, that is, Christ."

- Engagement with Culture: The church engages with culture, seeking to transform it through the gospel. Colossians 4:5-6 encourages, "Be wise in the way you act toward outsiders; make the most of every opportunity. Let your conversation be always full of grace, seasoned with salt, so that you may know how to answer everyone."

- Social Action: The church's witness includes social action, addressing issues of justice and compassion. Micah 6:8 declares, "He has shown you, O mortal, what is good. And what does the Lord require of you? To act justly and to love mercy and to walk humbly with your God."

8.2.5 Conclusion

The purpose of the church is multifaceted, encompassing worship, edification, evangelism, and witness. The church exists to glorify God, build up believers, spread the gospel, and reflect God's grace and truth to the world. Understanding these purposes provides clarity and direction for the church's mission and activities.

As the body of Christ, the bride of Christ, and the temple of the Holy Spirit, the church is called to fulfill its God-given purposes with faithfulness and zeal. By doing so, the church participates in God's redemptive plan and contributes to the transformation of individuals and societies. As we continue to explore systematic theology, the doctrine of the church's purpose remains central to understanding its role in God's mission and the believer's calling within the community of faith.

8.3 The Sacraments

The doctrine of the sacraments is an integral aspect of ecclesiology, examining the practices that signify and seal the promises of God to His people. The church observes two primary sacraments: baptism and the Lord's Supper. These sacraments are not merely symbolic rituals; they are means of grace that deepen the believer's faith and connection to Christ. In this chapter, we will explore the biblical basis, theological significance, and practical implications of these sacraments.

8.3.1 Baptism

Baptism is the sacrament of initiation into the Christian faith. It symbolizes the believer's identification with Christ's death and resurrection and serves as a public declaration of faith.

8.3.1.1 Biblical Basis for Baptism

The institution of baptism by Jesus Christ is recorded in the Great Commission. Matthew 28:19 states, "Therefore go and make disciples of all nations, baptizing them in the name of the Father and of the Son and of the Holy Spirit." This command underscores baptism's role in the process of discipleship.

Romans 6:3-4 further explains the significance of baptism: "Or don't you know that all of us who were baptized into Christ Jesus were baptized into His death? We were therefore buried with Him through baptism into death in order that, just as Christ was raised from the dead through the glory of the Father, we too may live a new life." Baptism signifies the believer's union with Christ in His death, burial, and resurrection.

8.3.1.2 Theological Significance of Baptism

- Union with Christ: Baptism signifies the believer's union with Christ. Galatians 3:27 states, "For all of you who were baptized into Christ have clothed yourselves with Christ." This union implies a new identity and a new way of life in Christ.

- Cleansing and Forgiveness: Baptism also symbolizes the cleansing from sin and the forgiveness granted through Christ. Acts 22:16 exhorts, "And now what are you waiting for? Get up, be baptized and wash your sins away, calling on His name."

- Entrance into the Covenant Community: Baptism marks the entrance into the covenant community of the church. 1 Corinthians 12:13 explains, "For we were all baptized by one Spirit so as to form one body—whether Jews or Gentiles, slave or free—and we were all given the one Spirit to drink."

8.3.1.3 Practical Implications of Baptism

- Public Declaration of Faith: Baptism serves as a public declaration of faith in Christ. It is a testimony to the believer's commitment to follow Jesus and an invitation for the church to provide support and accountability.

- Incorporation into the Church: Baptism incorporates the believer into the local and universal church. It signifies membership in the body of Christ and the beginning of a life of discipleship and service.

- Ongoing Significance: Baptism has ongoing significance as a reminder of the believer's identity in Christ. It encourages believers to live out their baptismal vows, pursuing holiness and faithful service to God.

8.3.2 The Lord's Supper

The Lord's Supper, also known as Communion or the Eucharist, is the sacrament of remembrance and fellowship. It commemorates Christ's sacrificial death and fosters unity among believers.

8.3.2.1 Biblical Basis for the Lord's Supper

The institution of the Lord's Supper is recorded in the Gospels. Matthew 26:26-28 recounts, "While they were eating, Jesus took bread, and when He had given thanks, He broke it and gave it to His disciples, saying, 'Take and eat; this is my body.' Then He took a cup, and when He had given thanks, He gave it to them, saying, 'Drink from it, all of you. This is my blood of the covenant, which is poured out for many for the forgiveness of sins.'"

1 Corinthians 11:23-26 provides further instruction on the practice: "For I received from the Lord what I also passed on to you: The Lord Jesus, on the night He was betrayed, took bread, and when He had given thanks, He broke it and said, 'This is my body, which is for you; do this in remembrance of me.' In the same way, after supper He took the cup, saying, 'This cup is the new covenant in my blood; do this, whenever you drink it, in remembrance of me.' For whenever you eat this bread and drink this cup, you proclaim the Lord's death until He comes."

8.3.2.2 Theological Significance of the Lord's Supper

- Remembrance of Christ's Sacrifice: The Lord's Supper is a remembrance of Christ's sacrificial death. It calls believers to reflect on the significance of His atonement and the grace that flows from His sacrifice.

- Participation in Christ's Body and Blood: The Lord's Supper signifies participation in the body and blood of Christ. 1 Corinthians 10:16 states, "Is not the cup of thanksgiving for which we give thanks a participation in the blood of Christ? And is not the bread that we break a participation in the body of Christ?"

- Proclamation of the Gospel: The Lord's Supper is a proclamation of the gospel. Each celebration declares the central truth of the Christian faith: Christ's death and resurrection for the forgiveness of sins.

- Anticipation of Christ's Return: The Lord's Supper also looks forward to Christ's return. 1 Corinthians 11:26 emphasizes, "For whenever you eat this bread and drink this cup, you proclaim the Lord's death until He comes."

8.3.2.3 Practical Implications of the Lord's Supper

- Spiritual Nourishment: The Lord's Supper provides spiritual nourishment for believers. It is a means of grace that strengthens faith and fosters spiritual growth.

- Unity and Fellowship: The Lord's Supper fosters unity and fellowship among believers. 1 Corinthians 10:17 explains, "Because there is one loaf, we, who are many, are one body, for we all share the one loaf." This sacrament emphasizes the communal nature of the Christian faith.

- Self-Examination and Repentance: The Lord's Supper calls believers to self-examination and repentance. 1 Corinthians 11:28 advises, "Everyone ought to examine themselves before they eat of the bread and drink from the cup." This practice promotes spiritual integrity and renewal.

- Thanksgiving and Worship: The Lord's Supper is an act of thanksgiving and worship. It provides an opportunity to give thanks for God's redemptive work in Christ and to worship Him for His love and grace.

8.3.3 The Relationship Between Baptism and the Lord's Supper

Baptism and the Lord's Supper are interconnected sacraments that together encapsulate the believer's initiation into the Christian faith and ongoing participation in the life of the church.

8.3.3.1 Initiation and Continuation

Baptism initiates the believer into the Christian faith, symbolizing the beginning of the new life in Christ. The Lord's Supper, on the other hand, is a continuing means of grace that sustains the believer in their spiritual journey. Together, these sacraments mark the start and ongoing nourishment of the Christian life.

8.3.3.2 Covenantal Signs

Both sacraments serve as covenantal signs. Baptism signifies entrance into the new covenant community, while the Lord's Supper signifies ongoing participation in the new covenant. They both point to the redemptive work of Christ and the believer's relationship with God.

8.3.3.3 Visible Words of the Gospel

Baptism and the Lord's Supper are often referred to as visible words of the gospel. They are tangible expressions of the grace and truth of the gospel, communicating the promises of God in a visible and experiential manner.

8.3.4 Conclusion

The sacraments of baptism and the Lord's Supper are central to the life and practice of the church. Baptism symbolizes the believer's identification with Christ's death and resurrection, marking their initiation into the Christian faith. The Lord's Supper commemorates Christ's sacrificial death, providing spiritual nourishment and fostering unity among believers.

These sacraments are means of grace that deepen the believer's faith and connection to Christ. They serve as covenantal signs, visible words of the gospel, and instruments of spiritual growth. Understanding and faithfully practicing these sacraments is essential for the church's mission and the believer's spiritual vitality.

As we continue to explore systematic theology, the doctrine of the sacraments remains central to our understanding of the church's purpose and the believer's relationship with God. Through baptism and the Lord's Supper, the church proclaims the gospel, nurtures faith, and anticipates the fulfillment of God's redemptive plan.

8.4 Church Government

The structure of church government is an essential aspect of ecclesiology, reflecting how a church organizes itself to fulfill its mission and ministry. Different Christian traditions have developed varying models of church government, including episcopal, presbyterian, and congregational systems. Each model seeks to align with biblical principles and promote effective ministry within the church. In this chapter, we will explore these three primary models of church government, their biblical foundations, and their practical implications.

8.4.1 Episcopal Church Government

The episcopal model of church government is characterized by a hierarchical structure with bishops holding significant authority over the church. This model is prevalent in Anglican, Roman Catholic, and Orthodox traditions.

8.4.1.1 Biblical Foundations

The episcopal model finds its biblical foundations in the roles of the apostles and early church leaders. The New Testament describes the appointment of elders (presbyters) and overseers (bishops) with authority over local congregations.

- Apostolic Leadership: The apostles exercised significant authority in the early church. Acts 15 describes the Jerusalem Council, where the apostles and elders made crucial decisions for the church.

- Bishops and Elders: The terms "bishop" (episkopos) and "elder" (presbyteros) are sometimes used interchangeably in the New Testament. For example, Titus 1:5-7 and Acts 20:17, 28 use these terms to describe church leaders. The role of Timothy and Titus as overseers of multiple churches in different cities suggests an early form of episcopal governance (1 Timothy 5:19-22; Titus 1:5).

8.4.1.2 Structure and Function

In the episcopal model, authority is centralized in the office of the bishop, who oversees multiple congregations and ordains clergy.

- Hierarchy: The hierarchy typically includes bishops, priests, and deacons. Bishops have authority over priests and deacons, and they ordain and supervise the clergy.

- Dioceses and Parishes: The church is divided into dioceses (geographical areas overseen by a bishop) and parishes (local congregations led by priests).

8.4.1.3 Practical Implications

- Unity and Continuity: The episcopal model promotes unity and continuity within the church by centralizing authority in the bishops, who ensure doctrinal consistency and oversee church discipline.

- Apostolic Succession: This model emphasizes apostolic succession, the belief that bishops are the successors of the apostles through an unbroken line of ordination. This succession is seen as a guarantee of the church's faithfulness to apostolic teaching.

8.4.2 Presbyterian Church Government

The presbyterian model of church government is characterized by a representative system where elders (presbyters) govern the church collectively. This model is common in Presbyterian and Reformed traditions.

8.4.2.1 Biblical Foundations

The presbyterian model draws its biblical support from the New Testament's emphasis on a plurality of elders governing the church.

- Plurality of Elders: The New Testament often describes church leadership as a plurality of elders. For example, Acts 14:23 states, "Paul and Barnabas appointed elders for them in each church and, with prayer and fasting, committed them to the Lord, in whom they had put their trust."

- Council of Elders: The council of elders in Acts 15 demonstrates a collective decision-making process. The apostles and elders in Jerusalem met to resolve doctrinal and practical issues, setting a precedent for presbyterian governance.

8.4.2.2 Structure and Function

In the presbyterian model, authority is vested in elected elders who govern the church at various levels.

- Session: The local church is governed by a session, a body of elected elders (both teaching and ruling elders). The pastor, or teaching elder, typically moderates the session.

- Presbytery: Multiple local churches are grouped into a presbytery, a regional body of elders that oversees the churches within its jurisdiction. The presbytery has the authority to ordain ministers and resolve disputes.

- General Assembly: The highest governing body in presbyterian polity is the general assembly, which represents the entire denomination and makes decisions on doctrinal, ethical, and administrative matters.

8.4.2.3 Practical Implications

- Shared Leadership: The presbyterian model emphasizes shared leadership and accountability among a plurality of elders, reducing the risk of autocratic rule.

- Representative Governance: This model ensures that decisions are made collectively, reflecting the diverse views of the church community and promoting unity through representative governance.

8.4.3 Congregational Church Government

The congregational model of church government is characterized by the autonomy of the local congregation. Each local church governs itself independently, often through democratic processes. This model is prevalent in Baptist, Congregationalist, and many non-denominational churches.

8.4.3.1 Biblical Foundations

The congregational model finds its biblical support in the New Testament's emphasis on the priesthood of all believers and the autonomy of local congregations.

- Priesthood of All Believers: 1 Peter 2:9 emphasizes the priesthood of all believers: "But you are a chosen people, a royal priesthood, a holy nation, God's special possession, that you may declare the praises of Him who called you out of darkness into His wonderful light." This concept supports the idea that all members have a role in church governance.

- Local Church Autonomy: The New Testament churches often functioned independently, making decisions as a local body. For example, Acts 6:3-6 describes the Jerusalem church selecting deacons to serve the community, indicating local decision-making.

8.4.3.2 Structure and Function

In the congregational model, each local church is self-governing and makes decisions through a democratic process involving its members.

- Congregational Meetings: The congregation holds regular meetings where members vote on significant decisions, such as the appointment of pastors, budget approval, and major ministry initiatives.

- Elders and Deacons: While the congregation as a whole holds final authority, many congregational churches elect elders and deacons to provide spiritual leadership and administrative support.

8.4.3.3 Practical Implications

- Local Autonomy: The congregational model emphasizes the autonomy and responsibility of the local church. Each congregation can adapt to its unique context and needs.

- Democratic Participation: This model promotes democratic participation, encouraging all members to be actively involved in decision-making and ministry.

8.4.4 Comparative Analysis and Conclusion

Each model of church government—episcopal, presbyterian, and congregational—has its strengths and challenges. The choice of church polity often reflects theological convictions, historical developments, and practical considerations.

8.4.4.1 Episcopal Model Strengths and Challenges

- Strengths: Promotes unity and continuity, ensures doctrinal consistency, and provides clear lines of authority.

- Challenges: Potential for hierarchical abuse, limited congregational involvement in decision-making.

8.4.4.2 Presbyterian Model Strengths and Challenges

- Strengths: Emphasizes shared leadership and accountability, ensures representative governance, and promotes unity through regional and national assemblies.

- Challenges: Complex governance structure, potential for bureaucratic inefficiency.

8.4.4.3 Congregational Model Strengths and Challenges

- Strengths: Emphasizes local autonomy and responsibility, encourages democratic participation, allows flexibility and adaptability.

- Challenges: Risk of congregational isolation, the potential for divisiveness, and lack of accountability.

Understanding the various models of church government helps believers appreciate the diversity within the body of Christ and the different ways churches seek to fulfill their mission. Each model strives to reflect biblical principles and promote effective ministry, contributing to the church's overall health and witness.

As we continue to explore systematic theology, the doctrine of church government remains central to understanding how the church organizes itself to carry out its mission and ministry in the world. Whether through episcopal, presbyterian, or congregational polity, the goal is to glorify God, edify believers, and evangelize the world, faithfully stewarding the responsibilities entrusted to the church.

CHAPTER 09

THE SECOND COMING OF CHRIST

9.1 The Second Coming of Christ

The second coming of Christ, also known as the Parousia, is a central tenet of Christian eschatology and hope. It is the anticipated return of Jesus Christ in glory to judge the living and the dead and to establish His eternal kingdom. This doctrine is foundational to the Christian faith, providing assurance of God's ultimate victory over sin and death and the consummation of His redemptive plan. In this chapter, we will explore the biblical basis, theological significance, and practical implications of the second coming of Christ.

9.1.1 Biblical Basis for the Second Coming

The New Testament is replete with references to the second coming of Christ, highlighting its importance and certainty.

9.1.1.1 The Promise of Christ's Return

Jesus Himself promised His return. In John 14:2-3, He assures His disciples, "My Father's house has many rooms; if that were not so, would I have told you that I am going there to prepare a place for you? And if I go and prepare a place for you, I will come back and take you to be with me that you also may be where I am." This promise underscores the personal and relational nature of His return.

9.1.1.2 Apostolic Teaching

The apostles consistently taught about the second coming of Christ. Paul's letters frequently address this doctrine. For instance, 1 Thessalonians 4:16-17 describes the event: "For the Lord Himself will come down from heaven, with a loud command, with the voice of the archangel and with the trumpet call of God, and the dead in Christ will rise first. After that, we who are still alive and are left will be caught up together with them in the clouds to meet the Lord in the air. And so we will be with the Lord forever." This passage emphasizes the dramatic and public nature of Christ's return.

9.1.1.3 Revelation and Prophecy

The book of Revelation provides a vivid depiction of Christ's return and the culmination of history. Revelation 19:11-16 portrays Christ as a victorious warrior king: "I saw heaven standing open and there before me was a white horse, whose rider is called Faithful and True. With justice He judges and wages war. His eyes are like blazing fire, and on His head are many crowns... On His robe and on His thigh He has this name written: king of kings and lord of lords." This imagery emphasizes Christ's authority and power.

9.1.2 Theological Significance of the Second Coming

The second coming of Christ is not only a future event but a doctrine rich with theological significance.

9.1.2.1 Fulfillment of Prophecy

The second coming of Christ fulfills numerous biblical prophecies. Throughout the Old and New Testaments, God's plan for history culminates in the return of His Son. Isaiah 9:7, for instance, prophesies about the reign of the Messiah: "Of the greatness of His government and peace there will be no end. He will reign on David's throne and over His kingdom, establishing and upholding it with justice and righteousness from that time on and forever."

9.1.2.2 Judgment and Justice

The second coming involves the final judgment of all people. 2 Timothy 4:1 states, "In the presence of God and of Christ Jesus, who will judge the living and the dead, and in view of His appearing and His kingdom, I give you this charge." This judgment will be righteous and just, addressing the deeds of all individuals.

9.1.2.3 Resurrection and Transformation

The second coming is closely linked with the resurrection of the dead and the transformation of believers. Philippians 3:20-21 explains, "But our citizenship is in heaven. And we eagerly await a Savior from there, the Lord Jesus Christ, who, by the power that enables Him to bring everything under His control, will transform our lowly bodies so that they will be like His glorious body." This transformation signifies the completion of salvation.

9.1.2.4 Establishment of the Kingdom

The second coming marks the full establishment of God's kingdom. Revelation 11:15 declares, "The seventh angel sounded his trumpet, and there were loud voices in heaven, which said: 'The kingdom of the world has become the kingdom of our Lord and of His Messiah, and He will reign forever and ever.'" This kingdom will be characterized by peace, righteousness, and the direct reign of Christ.

9.1.3 Practical Implications of the Second Coming

Belief in the second coming of Christ profoundly impacts the life and practice of believers.

9.1.3.1 Hope and Encouragement

The anticipation of Christ's return provides hope and encouragement, especially in times of suffering and persecution. Titus 2:13 calls believers to "wait for the blessed hope—the appearing of the glory of our great God and Savior, Jesus Christ." This hope sustains believers, reminding them of the future restoration and reward.

9.1.3.2 Ethical Living

The expectation of Christ's return motivates ethical and holy living. 1 John 3:2-3 states, "Dear friends, now we are children of God, and what we will be has not yet been made known. But we know that when Christ appears, we shall be like Him, for we shall see Him as He is. All who have this hope in Him purify themselves, just as He is pure." Believers are called to live in a manner worthy of their calling, reflecting Christ's character.

9.1.3.3 Vigilance and Readiness

Believers are urged to be vigilant and ready for Christ's return. Matthew 24:42-44 warns, "Therefore keep watch because you do not know on what day your Lord will come. But understand this: If the owner of the house had known at what time of night the thief was coming, he would have kept watch and would not have let his house be broken into. So you also must be ready, because the Son of Man will come at an hour when you do not expect Him." This readiness involves spiritual alertness and faithful stewardship.

9.1.3.4 Evangelism and Mission

The second coming intensifies the urgency of evangelism and mission. Matthew 28:19-20, the Great Commission, is given in the context of Christ's authority and His eventual return: "Therefore go and make disciples of all nations, baptizing them in the name of the Father and of the Son and of the Holy Spirit, and teaching them to obey everything I have commanded you. And surely I am with you always, to the very end of the age." Believers are compelled to share the gospel, knowing that Christ's return signifies the end of the opportunity for salvation.

9.1.4 Challenges and Interpretations

The doctrine of the second coming has been interpreted in various ways throughout church history, leading to different eschatological perspectives.

9.1.4.1 Pre-Millennialism

Pre-millennialism posits that Christ will return before a literal thousand-year reign on earth. This view is based on a literal interpretation of Revelation 20:1-6. Pre-millennialists believe that Christ's return will precede a period of peace and righteousness, followed by a final rebellion and the ultimate judgment.

9.1.4.2 Post-Millennialism

Post-millennialism holds that Christ will return after a symbolic millennium, a period during which the world will be progressively Christianized. This perspective emphasizes the triumph of the gospel and the establishment of God's kingdom on earth through the church's mission before Christ's return.

9.1.4.3 Amillennialism

Amillennialism interprets the millennium symbolically, viewing it as the current church age during which Christ reigns spiritually through His people. Amillennialists believe that Christ's return will coincide with the final judgment and the inauguration of the new heavens and new earth.

9.1.5 Conclusion

The second coming of Christ is a cornerstone of Christian eschatology, offering believers hope and assurance of God's ultimate victory over sin and death. This doctrine is grounded in the promises of Jesus, the teachings of the apostles, and the prophetic visions of Revelation. The second coming involves Christ's return in glory, the resurrection and transformation of believers, the final judgment, and the establishment of God's eternal kingdom.

Understanding the second coming motivates believers to live in hope, holiness, vigilance, and mission. While interpretations of the timing and nature of the millennium may vary, the certainty of Christ's return remains a unifying and essential aspect of the Christian faith. As we continue to explore systematic theology, the doctrine of the second coming remains central to our understanding of God's redemptive plan and the ultimate destiny of individuals and the world.

9.2 The Resurrection of the Dead

The resurrection of the dead is a fundamental doctrine of Christian eschatology, affirming that believers will be raised with glorified bodies, fit for eternal life in God's presence. This doctrine underscores the victory of God over sin and death, providing hope and assurance to believers regarding their future. In this chapter, we will explore the biblical basis, theological significance, and practical implications of the resurrection of the dead.

9.2.1 Biblical Basis for the Resurrection

The resurrection of the dead is a consistent theme throughout Scripture, with numerous passages in both the Old and New Testaments affirming this hope.

9.2.1.1 Old Testament Foundations

The concept of resurrection appears in several Old Testament texts. Daniel 12:2, for instance, declares, "Multitudes who sleep in the dust of the earth will awake: some to everlasting life, others to shame and everlasting contempt." This passage emphasizes the resurrection of both the righteous and the wicked.

Job also expresses hope in the resurrection. Job 19:25-27 states, "I know that my redeemer lives and that in the end, He will stand on the earth. And after my skin has been destroyed, yet in my flesh I will see God; I myself will see Him with my own eyes—I, and not another. How my heart yearns within me!" Job's affirmation of seeing God in his flesh reflects an early belief in bodily resurrection.

9.2.1.2 New Testament Fulfillment

The New Testament provides a fuller revelation of the resurrection, centered on the resurrection of Jesus Christ as the firstfruits of those who have fallen asleep.

- Jesus' Teachings: Jesus taught about the resurrection of the dead. In John 11:25-26, He states, "I am the resurrection and the life. The one who believes in me will live, even though they die; and whoever lives by believing in me will never die. Do you believe this?" Jesus' resurrection is the guarantee of believers' future resurrection.

- Paul's Teachings: The Apostle Paul elaborates on the resurrection in his epistles. 1 Corinthians 15 is a comprehensive chapter on this doctrine. Verses 42-44 explain, "So will it be with the resurrection of the dead. The body that is sown is perishable, it is raised imperishable; it is sown in dishonor, it is raised in glory; it is sown in weakness, it is raised in power; it is sown a natural body, it is raised a spiritual body." This passage highlights the transformation from perishable to imperishable, from dishonor to glory, from weakness to power, and from natural to spiritual.

- Resurrection of Christ: The resurrection of Jesus is central to the Christian faith and serves as the prototype for the believer's resurrection. 1 Corinthians 15:20-22 affirms, "But Christ has indeed been raised from the dead, the first fruits of those who have fallen asleep. For since death came through a man, the resurrection of the dead comes also through a man. For as in Adam all die, so in Christ all will be made alive."

9.2.2 Theological Significance of the Resurrection

The resurrection of the dead carries profound theological significance, emphasizing God's power, justice, and the hope of eternal life.

9.2.2.1 God's Victory Over Sin and Death

The resurrection demonstrates God's ultimate victory over sin and death. 1 Corinthians 15:54-57 proclaims, "When the perishable has been clothed with the imperishable, and the mortal with immortality, then the saying that is written will come true: 'Death has been swallowed up in victory.' 'Where, O death, is your victory? Where, O death, is your sting?' The sting of death is sin, and the power of sin is the law. But thanks be to God! He gives us the victory through our Lord Jesus Christ." The resurrection nullifies the power of death and affirms the triumph of life in Christ.

9.2.2.2 Affirmation of God's Justice

The resurrection also affirms God's justice. Acts 17:31 states, "For He has set a day when He will judge the world with justice by the man He has appointed. He has given proof of this to everyone by raising Him from the dead." The resurrection ensures that all people will face judgment, and justice will be perfectly executed.

9.2.2.3 Hope of Eternal Life

The resurrection provides believers with the hope of eternal life. Romans 6:5 declares, "For if we have been united with Him in a death like His, we will certainly also be united with Him in a resurrection like His." This hope sustains believers, assuring them of their future with God in His eternal kingdom.

9.2.3 The Nature of the Resurrected Body

The resurrection involves the transformation of the believer's body, making it fit for eternal life in God's presence.

9.2.3.1 Imperishable and Glorious

The resurrected body is imperishable and glorious. 1 Corinthians 15:42-43 states, "The body that is sown is perishable, it is raised imperishable; it is sown in dishonor, it is raised in glory; it is sown in weakness, it is raised in power." This transformation signifies a body that is free from decay, disease, and death, reflecting the glory of God.

9.2.3.2 Powerful and Spiritual

The resurrected body is also powerful and spiritual. 1 Corinthians 15:44 describes it as "sown a natural body, it is raised a spiritual body." This does not mean the body is immaterial but rather that it is empowered and animated by the Holy Spirit, perfectly suited for the new creation.

9.2.3.3 Continuity and Discontinuity

There is both continuity and discontinuity between the present body and the resurrected body. Philippians 3:21 explains, "who, by the power that enables Him to bring everything under His control, will transform our lowly bodies so that they will be like His glorious body." The resurrected body maintains a connection to the present body but is radically transformed to reflect Christ's glorified state.

9.2.4 Practical Implications of the Resurrection

The doctrine of the resurrection of the dead has significant practical implications for the believer's life, ethics, and hope.

9.2.4.1 Hope and Encouragement

The hope of resurrection provides encouragement in the face of suffering and death. 1 Thessalonians 4:13-14 comforts believers: "Brothers and sisters, we do not want you to be uninformed about those who sleep in death, so that you do not grieve like the rest of mankind, who have no hope. For we believe that Jesus died and rose again, and so we believe that God will bring with Jesus those who have fallen asleep in Him." This hope assures believers of a future reunion with Christ and their loved ones in the faith.

9.2.4.2 Motivation for Holy Living

The certainty of resurrection motivates believers to live holy and righteous lives. 1 Corinthians 15:58 exhorts, "Therefore, my dear brothers and sisters, stand firm. Let nothing move you. Always give yourselves fully to the work of the Lord, because you know that your labor in the Lord is not in vain." The promise of resurrection and eternal life inspires believers to persevere in their faith and service to God.

9.2.4.3 Perspective on Death

The doctrine of resurrection transforms the believer's perspective on death. Philippians 1:21 expresses, "For to me, to live is Christ and to die is gain." Death is no longer a cause for fear but a transition to eternal life with God. This perspective enables believers to face death with confidence and peace.

9.2.4.4 Engagement in Mission

The hope of resurrection encourages believers to engage in mission and evangelism. 2 Corinthians 5:20-21 declares, "We are therefore Christ's ambassadors, as though God were making His appeal through us. We implore you on Christ's behalf: Be reconciled to God. God made Him who had no sin to be sin for us, so that in Him we might become the righteousness of God." The promise of resurrection drives the mission to share the gospel, inviting others to participate in the hope of eternal life.

9.2.5 Conclusion

The resurrection of the dead is a cornerstone of Christian faith and hope, affirming that believers will be raised with glorified bodies, fit for eternal life in God's presence. This doctrine is grounded in the resurrection of Jesus Christ, the firstfruits of those who have fallen asleep, and it underscores God's victory over sin and death, His justice, and the hope of eternal life.

Understanding the resurrection of the dead has profound theological and practical implications. It provides hope and encouragement, motivates holy living, transforms the perspective on death, and drives engagement in mission.

As we continue to explore systematic theology, the doctrine of the resurrection remains central to our understanding of God's redemptive plan and the ultimate destiny of believers.

The promise of resurrection assures believers of their future with God, where they will experience the fullness of His glory and the joy of eternal life. This hope sustains and empowers believers to live faithfully, confident in the victory of Christ and the fulfillment of His promises.

9.3 The Final Judgment

The doctrine of the final judgment is a pivotal aspect of Christian eschatology. It teaches that all people will stand before God to give an account of their lives. This judgment will determine the eternal destinies of individuals: the righteous will inherit eternal life, while the wicked will face eternal separation from God. Understanding the final judgment is crucial for grasping the fullness of God's justice and mercy. In this chapter, we will explore the biblical basis, theological significance, and practical implications of the final judgment.

9.3.1 Biblical Basis for the Final Judgment

The concept of the final judgment is thoroughly grounded in Scripture, spanning both the Old and New Testaments.

9.3.1.1 Old Testament Foundations

The Old Testament prophets frequently spoke of a future day of judgment. For instance, Ecclesiastes 12:14 states, "For God will bring every deed into judgment, including every hidden thing, whether it is good or evil." This verse emphasizes the comprehensive nature of God's judgment.

Daniel 12:2 also addresses the final judgment: "Multitudes who sleep in the dust of the earth will awake: some to everlasting life, others to shame and everlasting contempt." This passage highlights the resurrection and subsequent judgment of both the righteous and the wicked.

9.3.1.2 New Testament Fulfillment

The New Testament provides a fuller revelation of the final judgment, particularly through the teachings of Jesus and the writings of the apostles.

- Jesus' Teachings: Jesus frequently taught about the final judgment. In Matthew 25:31-46, He describes the separation of the righteous and the wicked: "When the Son of Man comes in His glory, and all the angels with Him, He will sit on His glorious throne. All the nations will be gathered before Him, and He will separate the people one from another as a shepherd separates the sheep from the goats." This passage underscores the inevitability and finality of the judgment.

- Apostolic Teaching: The apostles also emphasized the final judgment. Paul, in Romans 14:10-12, writes, "For we will all stand before God's judgment seat. It is written: 'As surely as I live,' says the Lord, 'every knee will bow before me; every tongue will acknowledge God.' So then, each of us will give an account of ourselves to God." This teaching highlights personal accountability before God.

9.3.1.3 Revelation and Prophecy

The book of Revelation provides vivid imagery of the final judgment. Revelation 20:11-15 describes the great white throne judgment: "Then I saw a great white throne and Him who was seated on it. The earth and the heavens fled from His presence, and there was no place for them. And I saw the dead, great and small, standing before the throne, and books were opened. Another book was opened, which is the book of life. The dead were judged according to what they had done as recorded in the books... Anyone whose name was not found written in the book of life was thrown into the lake of fire." This passage emphasizes the thoroughness and justice of God's final judgment.

9.3.2 Theological Significance of the Final Judgment

The final judgment carries profound theological significance, reflecting God's justice, mercy, and the ultimate fulfillment of His redemptive plan.

9.3.2.1 Divine Justice

The final judgment demonstrates God's perfect justice. Romans 2:6-8 states, "God 'will repay each person according to what they have done.' To those who by persistence in doing good seek glory, honor, and immortality, He will give eternal life. But for those who are self-seeking and who reject the truth and follow evil, there will be wrath and anger." God's judgment is impartial and righteous, ensuring that justice is served for every deed.

9.3.2.2 Divine Mercy

The final judgment also highlights God's mercy toward the righteous. John 5:24 promises, "Very truly I tell you, whoever hears my word and believes Him who sent me has eternal life and will not be judged but has crossed over from death to life." Believers, through faith in Christ, receive mercy and are granted eternal life.

9.3.2.3 Fulfillment of God's Redemptive Plan

The final judgment is the culmination of God's redemptive plan. It marks the end of history as we know it and the beginning of the eternal state. Revelation 21:1-4 describes the new heavens and the new earth: "Then I saw 'a new heaven and a new earth,' for the first heaven and the first earth had passed away, and there was no longer any sea. I saw the Holy City, the new Jerusalem, coming down out of heaven from God, prepared as a bride beautifully dressed for her husband. And I heard a loud voice from the throne saying, 'Look! God's dwelling place is now among the people, and He will dwell with them. They will be His people, and God Himself will be with them and be their God. He will wipe every tear from their eyes. There will be no more death' or mourning or crying or pain, for the old order of things has passed away.'" This vision encapsulates the ultimate renewal and restoration of creation.

9.3.3 Practical Implications of the Final Judgment

The doctrine of the final judgment has significant practical implications for believers, influencing their ethics, worship, and mission.

9.3.3.1 Ethical Living

The certainty of the final judgment motivates ethical living. 2 Corinthians 5:10-11 states, "For we must all appear before the judgment seat of Christ, so that each of us may receive what is due us for the things done while in the body, whether good or bad. Since, then, we know what it is to fear the Lord, we try to persuade others." Believers are encouraged to live righteously, knowing they will give an account of their lives.

9.3.3.2 Worship and Reverence

The doctrine of the final judgment fosters worship and reverence for God. Hebrews 12:28-29 exhorts, "Therefore, since we are receiving a kingdom that cannot be shaken, let us be thankful, and so worship God acceptably with reverence and awe, for our 'God is a consuming fire.'" Recognizing God's holiness and justice leads to a deeper sense of reverence and gratitude in worship.

9.3.3.3 Evangelism and Mission

The impending final judgment underscores the urgency of evangelism and mission. 2 Peter 3:9-10 reminds believers of God's patience and the need for repentance: "The Lord is not slow in keeping His promise, as some understand slowness. Instead, He is patient with you, not wanting anyone to perish, but everyone to come to repentance. But the day of the Lord will come like a thief." This knowledge compels believers to share the gospel, inviting others to receive God's mercy and avoid His wrath.

9.3.3.4 Comfort and Hope

For believers, the final judgment offers comfort and hope. Romans 8:1 assures, "Therefore, there is now no condemnation for those who are in Christ Jesus." This promise provides confidence and peace, knowing that through Christ, believers are justified and will inherit eternal life.

9.3.4 Challenges and Interpretations

The doctrine of the final judgment has been interpreted in various ways, leading to different eschatological perspectives.

9.3.4.1 Universalism

Universalism posits that ultimately, all people will be saved and reconciled to God. This view, however, is not supported by traditional Christian theology, which upholds the clear biblical teaching of eternal separation for the wicked as seen in Matthew 25:46: "Then they will go away to eternal punishment, but the righteous to eternal life."

9.3.4.2 Annihilationism

Annihilationism teaches that the wicked will be ultimately destroyed rather than subjected to eternal conscious punishment. Proponents of this view interpret passages like Matthew 10:28, which states, "Do not be afraid of those who kill the body but cannot kill the soul. Rather, be afraid of the One who can destroy both soul and body in hell." They argue that "destruction" implies a final end rather than eternal torment. However, traditional Christian theology often counters this with texts like Revelation 14:11, which describes the torment of the wicked as continuing "forever and ever."

9.3.4.3 Conditional Immortality

Conditional immortality is the belief that only the righteous will be granted eternal life, while the wicked will be annihilated after the final judgment. This view holds that immortality is not inherent to all souls but is a gift bestowed upon believers. Advocates of this perspective point to verses like John 3:16, which speaks of eternal life as a gift from God, contrasted with perishing for the unbeliever.

9.3.5 Conclusion

The doctrine of the final judgment is a cornerstone of Christian eschatology, affirming that all people will stand before God to give an account of their lives. This judgment will determine the eternal destinies of individuals: the righteous will inherit eternal life, while the wicked will face eternal separation from God. Understanding the final judgment is crucial for comprehending the fullness of God's justice and mercy.

The final judgment demonstrates God's perfect justice and mercy, culminating in the ultimate fulfillment of His redemptive plan. This doctrine has profound theological significance, providing hope and assurance to believers and emphasizing the need for righteous living, worship, and mission.

The practical implications of the final judgment include motivating ethical living, fostering worship and reverence, underscoring the urgency of evangelism and mission, and offering comfort and hope to believers. While there are various interpretations of the final judgment, the traditional Christian understanding affirms eternal life for the righteous and eternal separation for the wicked.

As we continue to explore systematic theology, the doctrine of the final judgment remains central to our understanding of God's redemptive plan and the ultimate destiny of humanity. The certainty of this judgment calls believers to live faithfully, share the gospel urgently, and worship God reverently, confident in His justice and mercy.

9.4 The New Heavens and New Earth

The doctrine of the new heavens and new earth is a profound aspect of Christian eschatology, offering a vision of the ultimate renewal and restoration of creation. This renewed creation, promised by God, will be free from sin, suffering, and death. Believers will enjoy unbroken fellowship with God forever. In this chapter, we will explore the biblical basis, theological significance, and practical implications of the new heavens and new earth.

9.4.1 Biblical Basis for the New Heavens and New Earth

The concept of a new heavens and new earth is deeply rooted in both the Old and New Testaments, culminating in the visions of the book of Revelation.

9.4.1.1 Old Testament Foundations

The prophet Isaiah spoke of a future renewed creation. Isaiah 65:17 declares, "See, I will create new heavens and a new earth. The former things will not be remembered, nor will they come to mind." This promise points to a complete transformation of the current order, bringing about a new and glorious reality.

Isaiah 66:22 further affirms, "As the new heavens and the new earth that I make will endure before me," declares the Lord, "so will your name and descendants endure." This enduring new creation is a testament to God's faithfulness and eternal covenant with His people.

9.4.1.2 New Testament Fulfillment

The New Testament provides a fuller revelation of the new heavens and new earth, particularly in the writings of Peter and John.

- Peter's Teaching: The Apostle Peter connects the promise of new creation with the return of Christ. 2 Peter 3:13 states, "But in keeping with His promise we are looking forward to a new heaven and a new earth, where righteousness dwells." This new creation is characterized by righteousness, in stark contrast to the current world marred by sin.

- John's Vision: The book of Revelation offers a detailed vision of the new heavens and new earth. Revelation 21:1-4 provides a vivid description: "Then I saw 'a new heaven and a new earth,' for the first heaven and the first earth had passed away, and there was no longer any sea. I saw the Holy City, the new Jerusalem, coming down out of heaven from God, prepared as a bride beautifully dressed for her husband. And I heard a loud voice from the throne saying, 'Look! God's dwelling place is now among the people, and He will dwell with them. They will be His people, and God Himself will be with them and be their God. He will wipe every tear from their eyes. There will be no more death' or mourning or crying or pain, for the old order of things has passed away.'" This passage highlights the elimination of suffering and the establishment of eternal fellowship with God.

9.4.2 Theological Significance of the New Heavens and New Earth

The new heavens and new earth hold profound theological significance, encapsulating the fulfillment of God's redemptive plan and the ultimate hope for believers.

9.4.2.1 Fulfillment of God's Promises

The new heavens and new earth represent the fulfillment of God's promises to renew and restore creation. Throughout Scripture, God's intention to redeem not only humanity but all of creation is evident. Romans 8:21-22 states, "that the creation itself will be liberated from its bondage to decay and brought into the freedom and glory of the children of God. We know that the whole creation has been groaning as in the pains of childbirth right up to the present time." The new creation fulfills this hope of liberation and renewal.

9.4.2.2 Restoration of Fellowship with God

In the new heavens and new earth, the separation caused by sin will be completely eradicated, and believers will experience unbroken fellowship with God. Revelation 21:3 declares, "And I heard a loud voice from the throne saying, 'Look! God's dwelling place is now among the people, and He will dwell with them. They will be His people, and God Himself will be with them and be their God.'" This intimate fellowship is the culmination of God's redemptive work.

9.4.2.3 Elimination of Sin, Suffering, and Death

The new creation will be free from the effects of sin, suffering, and death. Revelation 21:4 emphasizes, "He will wipe every tear from their eyes. There will be no more death' or mourning or crying or pain, for the old order of things has passed away." This complete renewal signifies the ultimate victory of God over all that corrupts and harms His creation.

9.4.2.4 Eternal Righteousness and Peace

The new heavens and new earth will be characterized by eternal righteousness and peace. Isaiah 11:6-9 portrays a harmonious creation where even natural enemies live in peace: "The wolf will live with the lamb, the leopard will lie down with the goat, the calf and the lion and the yearling together; and a little child will lead them... They will neither harm nor destroy on all my holy mountain, for the earth will be filled with the knowledge of the Lord as the waters cover the sea." This vision represents the perfect shalom (peace) that will pervade the new creation.

9.4.3 Practical Implications of the New Heavens and New Earth

The doctrine of the new heavens and new earth has significant practical implications for the life and faith of believers.

9.4.3.1 Hope and Encouragement

The promise of a new heavens and new earth provides profound hope and encouragement. 2 Peter 3:13 reminds believers to look forward to this new creation: "But in keeping with His promise we are looking forward to a new heaven and a new earth, where righteousness dwells." This hope sustains believers through present trials and sufferings, assuring them of a glorious future.

9.4.3.2 Motivation for Holy Living

The anticipation of the new creation motivates believers to live holy and godly lives. 2 Peter 3:11-12 urges, "Since everything will be destroyed in this way, what kind of people ought you to be? You ought to live holy and godly lives as you look forward to the day of God and speed its coming." The certainty of God's future renewal encourages ethical living and spiritual readiness.

9.4.3.3 Stewardship of Creation

The hope of a new creation calls believers to responsible stewardship of the current creation. While the new heavens and new earth will be a complete renewal, caring for God's creation now reflects His original intent and anticipates the coming restoration. Genesis 2:15 illustrates this stewardship: "The Lord God took the man and put him in the Garden of Eden to work it and take care of it."

9.4.3.4 Witness to the World

The promise of a renewed creation enhances the church's witness to the world. It provides a compelling vision of God's ultimate plan, inviting others to participate in this hope. Revelation 22:17 extends this invitation: "The Spirit and the bride say, 'Come!' And let the one who hears say, 'Come!'

Let the one who is thirsty come; and let the one who wishes take the free gift of the water of life."

9.4.4 Challenges and Interpretations

The doctrine of the new heavens and new earth has been interpreted in various ways, reflecting different eschatological perspectives.

9.4.4.1 Literal and Symbolic Interpretations

Some theologians interpret the descriptions of the new heavens and new earth literally, expecting a physical transformation of the universe. Others view these descriptions symbolically, representing the spiritual realities of God's ultimate renewal. Both perspectives emphasize the profound change that will occur in God's new creation.

9.4.4.2 Continuity and Discontinuity

Debates also arise over the continuity and discontinuity between the present creation and the new creation. Some argue for significant continuity, seeing the new creation as a restoration of the original creation's goodness. Others emphasize discontinuity, focusing on the radical newness of the renewed creation. This tension reflects the balance between God's redemption of the current creation and the introduction of a wholly transformed reality.

9.4.5 Conclusion

The doctrine of the new heavens and new earth is a cornerstone of Christian eschatology, offering a vision of the ultimate renewal and restoration of creation. This renewed creation, promised by God, will be free from sin, suffering, and death. Believers will enjoy unbroken fellowship with God forever.

The new heavens and new earth hold profound theological significance, fulfilling God's promises, restoring fellowship with Him, eliminating the effects of sin, and establishing eternal righteousness and peace. Understanding this doctrine provides hope and encouragement, motivates holy living, calls for responsible stewardship, and enhances the church's witness to the world.

As we continue to explore systematic theology, the doctrine of the new heavens and new earth remains central to our understanding of God's redemptive plan and the ultimate destiny of creation. This promise assures believers of a glorious future with God, where they will experience the fullness of His presence and the perfection of His creation, living in eternal peace and righteousness.

CONCLUSION

Systematic theology provides a structured approach to understanding the vast and profound truths of the Christian faith. By systematically studying and embracing these doctrines, believers can grow in their knowledge of God, deepen their faith, and live out their calling with greater clarity and conviction. The journey of theological exploration is both intellectually enriching and spiritually transformative, leading us to a deeper love for God and a more faithful witness to His grace and truth.

10.1 The Importance of Systematic Theology

Systematic theology is essential for several reasons. It helps believers organize and articulate their beliefs, ensures doctrinal integrity, and fosters spiritual growth.

10.1.1 Organizing and Articulating Beliefs

Systematic theology helps believers organize the teachings of Scripture into coherent categories, making it easier to understand and articulate the Christian faith. By studying doctrines such as the nature of God, Christology, soteriology, and eschatology, believers can develop a comprehensive understanding of what they believe and why they believe it. This structured approach equips believers to explain their faith clearly and confidently to others.

10.1.2 Ensuring Doctrinal Integrity

Systematic theology guards against false teachings and doctrinal errors by grounding beliefs in the consistent and comprehensive study of Scripture. By comparing and synthesizing biblical texts, systematic theology helps ensure that our understanding of God's revelation is faithful to the entirety of Scripture. This process helps maintain the purity of the gospel and the integrity of the Christian faith.

10.1.3 Fostering Spiritual Growth

Studying systematic theology is not merely an intellectual exercise; it is a means of fostering spiritual growth. As believers delve into the deep truths of God's word, their faith is strengthened, their love for God is deepened, and their lives are transformed. Systematic theology encourages believers to live out their faith with greater conviction and passion, impacting their personal lives and their witness to the world.

10.2 Key Doctrines Explored

Throughout this exploration of systematic theology, we have examined key doctrines that form the foundation of the Christian faith. Each doctrine provides essential insights into God's character, His work, and His purposes for humanity and creation.

10.2.1 The Doctrine of Revelation

The doctrine of revelation explains how God communicates with humanity. Through general revelation (nature and conscience) and special revelation (Scripture and Jesus Christ), God makes Himself known. This foundational doctrine affirms the reliability and authority of the Bible, guiding believers in their understanding of God's will and truth.

10.2.2 The Doctrine of God

The doctrine of God explores the nature, attributes, and works of God. Understanding God's character—His holiness, love, justice, omnipotence, and omniscience—provides a foundation for worship and obedience. The doctrine of the Trinity, which reveals God as Father, Son, and Holy Spirit, underscores the complexity and unity of God's being.

10.2.3 The Doctrine of Christ

Christology focuses on the person and work of Jesus Christ. The doctrines of the incarnation, atonement, resurrection, and ascension highlight the significance of Christ's mission to redeem humanity. Jesus' dual nature as fully God and fully man is essential for understanding His role as the mediator between God and humanity.

10.2.4 The Doctrine of the Holy Spirit

The doctrine of the Holy Spirit examines the Spirit's person and work in the life of believers and the church. The Holy Spirit's roles in regeneration, sanctification, empowerment, and guidance are crucial for spiritual growth and effective ministry. The gifts and fruit of the Spirit demonstrate the transformative work of God in believers' lives.

10.2.5 The Doctrine of Salvation

Soteriology explores the process of salvation, including election, calling, regeneration, justification, sanctification, and glorification. Understanding these stages helps believers appreciate the depth of God's grace and the assurance of their salvation. The doctrine of salvation emphasizes God's initiative and the believer's response of faith and repentance.

10.2.6 The Doctrine of the Church

Ecclesiology examines the nature, purpose, and mission of the church. The church is described as the body of Christ, the bride of Christ, and the temple of the Holy Spirit.

These metaphors highlight the church's unity, holiness, and purpose in worship, edification, evangelism, and service. Different models of church government—episcopal, presbyterian, and congregational—reflect diverse approaches to organizing the church for effective ministry.

10.2.7 The Doctrine of Last Things

Eschatology explores the ultimate destiny of individuals and the world according to God's redemptive plan. Key aspects include the second coming of Christ, the resurrection of the dead, the final judgment, and the new heavens and new earth. These doctrines provide hope and assurance of God's ultimate victory over sin and death, and they encourage believers to live with an eternal perspective.

10.3 The Transformative Power of Theology

Engaging in systematic theology is transformative. It shapes not only our understanding but also our character, relationships, and mission. Theology that remains theoretical and detached from life fails to achieve its purpose. True theology is lived out in daily practice.

10.3.1 Shaping Character

The study of theology transforms our character by aligning our hearts and minds with God's truth. As we understand God's holiness, we are called to live holy lives. As we grasp God's love, we are moved to love others sacrificially.

Theology shapes our values, priorities, and actions, conforming us to the image of Christ.

10.3.2 Strengthening Relationships

Theological understanding strengthens our relationships within the church and with the world. A deeper grasp of doctrines such as the Trinity and the body of Christ fosters unity and mutual support among believers. Theology also equips us to engage with others compassionately and wisely, sharing the gospel and addressing contemporary issues from a biblical perspective.

10.3.3 Empowering Mission

The study of theology empowers believers for mission. Understanding the doctrines of revelation, salvation, and eschatology equips us to share the gospel effectively and to serve with hope and perseverance. Theology provides the foundation for engaging the world with truth and grace, fulfilling the Great Commission and living out our calling to be salt and light.

10.4 A Lifelong Journey

Systematic theology is not a one-time study but a lifelong journey. The depths of God's truth are inexhaustible, and our understanding continually grows as we study Scripture, engage with the community of faith, and experience God's work in our lives.

10.4.1 Continuous Learning

Believers are called to continuous learning and growth in their understanding of God. 2 Peter 3:18 encourages, "But grow in the grace and knowledge of our Lord and Savior Jesus Christ. To Him be glory both now and forever! Amen." This pursuit of knowledge is an ongoing process that deepens our relationship with God and our effectiveness in His service.

10.4.2 Community Engagement

The journey of theological exploration is best undertaken within the context of community. Engaging with the diverse perspectives and experiences of fellow believers enriches our understanding and challenges us to grow. The church provides a vital environment for theological discussion, discipleship, and mutual edification.

10.4.3 Dependence on the Holy Spirit

Throughout this journey, believers rely on the guidance and illumination of the Holy Spirit. John 16:13 promises, "But when He, the Spirit of truth, comes, He will guide you into all the truth." The Holy Spirit helps us understand and apply God's word, leading us into a deeper knowledge of Him and empowering us for faithful living.

10.5 Conclusion

Systematic theology is a structured and comprehensive approach to understanding the profound truths of the Christian faith. By studying and embracing these doctrines, believers grow in their knowledge of God, deepen their faith, and live out their calling with greater clarity and conviction. The journey of theological exploration is both intellectually enriching and spiritually transformative, leading us to a deeper love for God and a more faithful witness to His grace and truth.

As we conclude this exploration of systematic theology, we are reminded that the ultimate goal of theology is not merely knowledge but worship. True theology leads us to a deeper adoration of God, a greater commitment to His purposes, and a more profound experience of His presence. May our study of theology continually draw us closer to God, transform our lives, and equip us to share His love and truth with the world.

STUDY QUESTIONS FOR EACH CHAPTER

Chapter 1: Introduction to Systematic Theology

1. What is systematic theology, and why is it important for understanding the Christian faith?

2. How does systematic theology differ from biblical theology and historical theology?

3. What are the main benefits of studying systematic theology?

4. How can systematic theology help believers articulate their faith more clearly?

Chapter 2: The Doctrine of Revelation

1. What are the two main types of revelation, and how do they differ?

2. How does the doctrine of inspiration affirm the authority and reliability of Scripture?

3. Why is inerrancy an essential aspect of the doctrine of Scripture?

4. How does special revelation complement and fulfill general revelation?

Chapter 3: The Doctrine of God

1. What are the key attributes of God, and why are they important for understanding His nature?

2. How does the doctrine of the Trinity reconcile the oneness of God with the three distinct persons?

3. In what ways does God's sovereignty impact our understanding of His providence and control over creation?

4. How can a deeper knowledge of God's attributes enhance our worship and trust in Him?

Chapter 4: The Doctrine of Christ

1. What is the significance of the hypostatic union in understanding the person of Jesus Christ?

2. How do the events of the incarnation, atonement, resurrection, and ascension each contribute to our salvation?

3. What roles does Christ fulfill as prophet, priest, and king, and why are these roles important?

4. How can a deeper understanding of Christology impact our faith and daily living?

Chapter 5: The Doctrine of the Holy Spirit

1. What are the primary roles of the Holy Spirit in the life of believers and the church?

2. How does the Holy Spirit contribute to the process of sanctification and spiritual growth?

3. What are the gifts of the Spirit, and how are they intended to be used within the church?

4. How can believers cultivate a more intimate relationship with the Holy Spirit?

Chapter 6: The Doctrine of Humanity

1. What does it mean to be created in the image of God, and how does this influence our understanding of human dignity and purpose?

2. How did the fall of humanity impact our nature and relationship with God?

3. What is the nature of sin, and how does it affect all aspects of human existence?

4. How does redemption and restoration through Christ address the consequences of the fall?

Chapter 7: The Doctrine of Salvation

1. What are the key stages in the process of salvation, and how do they relate to one another?

2. How does the doctrine of justification by faith alone provide assurance of salvation?

3. What is the role of sanctification in the life of a believer, and how is it different from justification?

4. How does the hope of glorification influence our present faith and conduct?

Chapter 8: The Doctrine of the Church

1. What are the primary purposes of the church, and how do they reflect God's mission?

2. How do baptism and the Lord's Supper function as sacraments within the church?

3. What are the different models of church government, and what are their respective strengths and challenges?

4. How can understanding the nature and mission of the church enhance our involvement and commitment to the local congregation?

Chapter 9: The Doctrine of Last Things

1. What is the significance of the second coming of Christ, and how does it shape our hope and expectation?

2. How does the doctrine of the resurrection of the dead affirm God's victory over sin and death?

3. What are the key elements of the final judgment, and how should this knowledge influence our lives?

4. What is the vision of the new heavens and new earth, and how does it fulfill God's redemptive plan?

Discussion Guides for Small Groups

Chapter 1: Introduction to Systematic Theology

- Discuss the different types of theology (systematic, biblical, historical) and their importance.

- Share personal experiences of how studying theology has impacted your faith.

- Consider practical ways to incorporate systematic theology into regular Bible study.

Chapter 2: The Doctrine of Revelation

- Explore the significance of both general and special revelation in knowing God.

- Discuss the importance of the inspiration and inerrancy of Scripture in daily life.

- Reflect on how the Bible has provided guidance and truth in your personal journey.

Chapter 3: The Doctrine of God

- Discuss the attributes of God and how they influence your understanding of His nature.

- Reflect on the mystery and importance of the Trinity.

- Share experiences of how a deeper knowledge of God's sovereignty and love has impacted your faith.

Chapter 4: The Doctrine of Christ

- Discuss the significance of the incarnation, atonement, resurrection, and ascension.

- Reflect on the different roles of Christ as prophet, priest, and king in your life.

- Consider how understanding Christology can strengthen your daily walk with Jesus.

Chapter 5: The Doctrine of the Holy Spirit

- Discuss the role of the Holy Spirit in the life of the believer and the church.

- Reflect on personal experiences of the Spirit's guidance and empowerment.

- Consider how the gifts and fruit of the Spirit are evident in your community.

Chapter 6: The Doctrine of Humanity

- Discuss the implications of being created in the image of God.

- Reflect on the impact of sin and the fall on humanity and personal life.

- Share how the hope of redemption and restoration through Christ has transformed your life.

Chapter 7: The Doctrine of Salvation

- Explore the stages of salvation and their importance in the Christian journey.

- Discuss the assurance provided by justification and the ongoing process of sanctification.

- Reflect on how the hope of glorification influences your present faith and actions.

Chapter 8: The Doctrine of the Church

- Discuss the purposes of the church and how they are reflected in your local congregation.

- Explore the significance of the sacraments of baptism and the Lord's Supper.

- Reflect on different models of church government and how they impact church life.

Chapter 9: The Doctrine of Last Things

- Discuss the significance of the second coming of Christ and its impact on Christian hope.

- Reflect on the resurrection of the dead and its affirmation of God's victory.

- Consider the implications of the final judgment and the vision of the new heavens and new earth for your life.

Additional Resources on Systematic Theology

Books

1. "Systematic Theology" by Wayne Grudem – A comprehensive and accessible introduction to systematic theology.

2. "Institutes of the Christian Religion" by John Calvin – A foundational text in Reformed theology, offering deep insights into Christian doctrine.

3. "Christian Theology" by Millard J. Erickson – A thorough exploration of theological topics from an evangelical perspective.

4. "A Theology for the Church" edited by Daniel L. Akin – A collection of essays by various theologians covering all major areas of theology.

Online Resources

1. The Gospel Coalition – Offers a wide range of articles, podcasts, and videos on theological topics and issues facing the church today.

2. Ligonier Ministries – Provides resources from a Reformed perspective, including teaching series, articles, and books on systematic theology.

3. Desiring God – Features articles, sermons, and resources by John Piper and others, focusing on God's glory and Christian living.

4. Blue Letter Bible – An online tool for Bible study, including commentaries, dictionaries, and theological resources.

Courses and Lectures

1. Reformed Theological Seminary (RTS) – Offers free online courses on systematic theology and other theological topics taught by respected scholars.

2. Biblical Training – Provides free access to a variety of theological courses and lectures from leading evangelical scholars.

3. The Great Courses – Features lecture series on theology and religious studies by university professors, available for purchase or streaming.

Podcasts

1. Ask Pastor John – John Piper answers theological and practical questions from listeners.

2. Renewing Your Mind – Daily podcast from Ligonier Ministries featuring teachings from R.C. Sproul and other theologians.

3. Theology in the Raw – Hosted by Preston Sprinkle, addressing contemporary theological issues and questions.

4. Core Christianity – Provides answers to listener questions about theology, doctrine, and Christian living.

Study Groups and Forums

1. Bible Study Fellowship (BSF) – An international organization offering structured Bible study groups, including doctrinal topics.

2. The Puritan Board – An online forum for discussing Reformed theology and related issues.

3. Christian Classics Ethereal Library (CCEL) – An online community and resource for studying classic Christian writings and theology.

Engaging with these resources can deepen your understanding of systematic theology and its application in your life and ministry. Whether through reading, discussion, or formal study, the pursuit of theological knowledge is a lifelong journey that enriches faith and fosters a closer relationship with God.

www.ingramcontent.com/pod-product-compliance
Lightning Source LLC
Chambersburg PA
CBHW061241120726
48001CB00001B/75